THE JEWLISH COOKBOOK

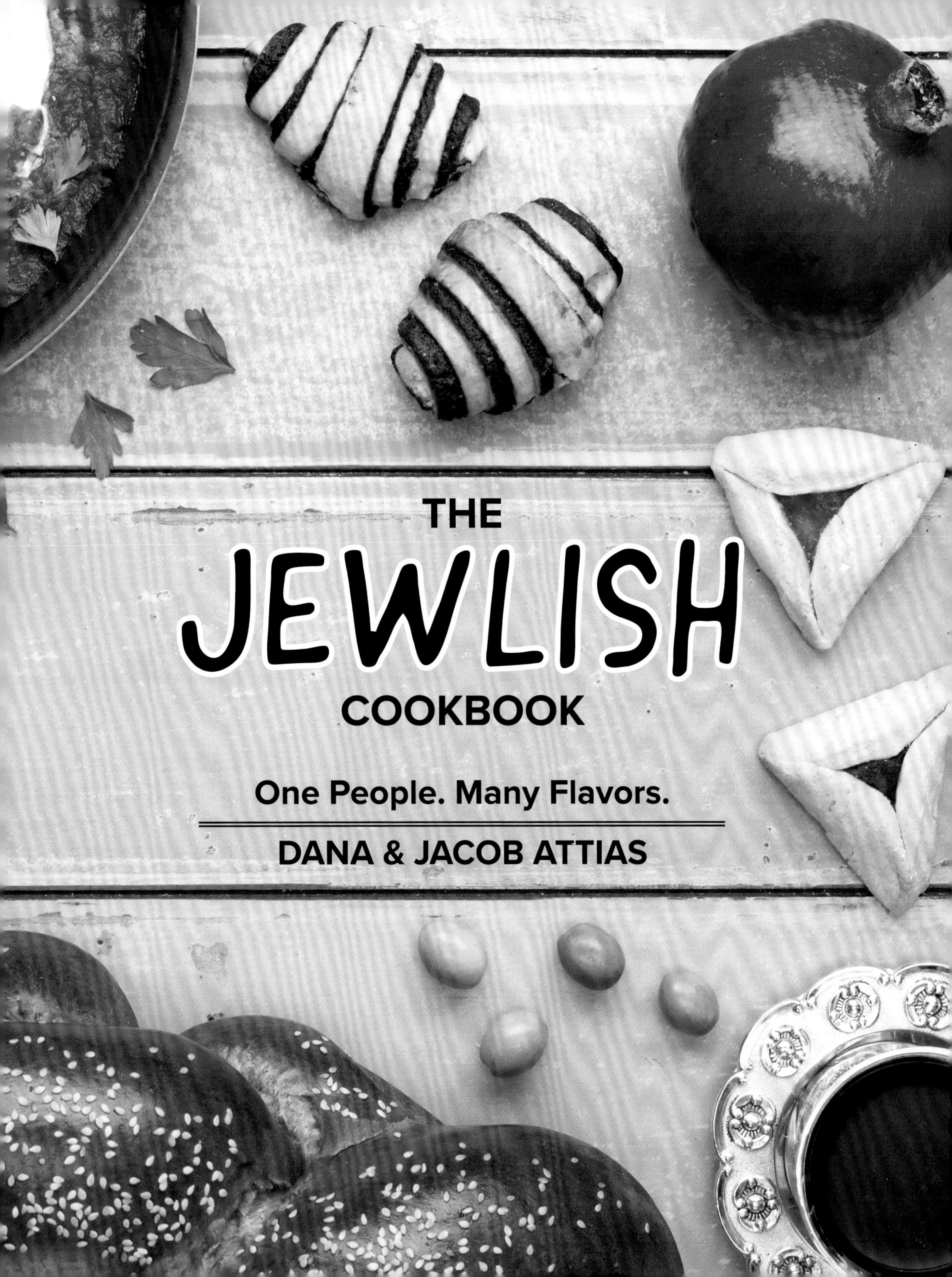
THE
JEWLISH
COOKBOOK
One People. Many Flavors.
DANA & JACOB ATTIAS

Printed in China

Design by Dana Attias
Photography by Jacob Attias
Text by Dana and Jacob Attias

For bulk purchase, tour, promotional and educational enquiries please contact us at info@jewlish.com

ISBN 978-0-692-90341-4

www.jewlish.com

First printing, August 2017

10 9 8 7 6 5 4 3 2 1

One People.
Many Flavors.

Contents

CHALLAH
DIPS
VEGETABLES
CHEESE
FISH
MEAT
HOLIDAYS
DESSERT

We know what you're thinking:

your grandmother's recipes are better. Yes, we've heard it all before. But since you'll never get the exact ingredients from her ("a pinch of this, a scoop of that"), you may as well dive right in.

The reason grandmothers never reveal their recipes is because they don't use recipes. They cook with their senses. They know if challah dough needs more flour just by its feel.

There's the Yiddish word *potchke* that means "to mess around," or "to waste time and effort." Apparently, our grandparents had plenty of time to *potchke* around in the kitchen, keep fish in the bathtub and peel tomatoes by hand. For us, with our busy schedules of work deadlines, gym memberships, Netflix and chilling, it's hard to find time to get to know our challah dough in the same way. So, with the desire and struggle to recreate the flavors that came out of our grandparent's kitchens – where do we even begin?

Jewlish began

six months after our wedding, in February 2016. We (Dana and Jacob) built a cooking studio in the middle of our tiny Tel Aviv apartment. Lights, camera, action! Our drool-worthy cooking videos began to go viral. To our surprise, hundreds of views turned into thousands and by the end of its first year, Jewlish reached over 50 million unique people! That's right, 50 million people hunched over their smartphones watching videos about Jewish cooking: classic recipes that our grandparents made and modern adaptations that keep to tradition yet inspire the busy millennial to find time to connect with their roots.

It might be a miracle that we even met.

Dana was raised in London and Jerusalem while Jacob grew up in Cleveland, Ohio (a place Dana had never heard of). Against all odds, and thanks to our inclinations to walk the road less travelled, we met at university in Israel. Being from different parts of the world, we had our differences, especially when it came to food. But these exciting differences drew us together.

Dana's family is Israeli-Spanish-Moroccan. They're the type that lives in the state of constant balagan* and enjoys every second of it. At their dinner table, if you want someone to pass the olives or the spicy fish, you're going to have to shout for it. Dana's Moroccan grandmother, Dolly, who we call 'Abuela', serves Spanish-Moroccan food that ranges from little marzipan cookies to more obscure Sephardic* dishes that most people haven't heard of, like Orisa, a sweet potato and barley Shabbat stew. Dana's Spanish-Moroccan heritage greatly influences the recipes we make for Jewlish.

1971 Tétouan*, Morocco
Dana's grandparents at a New Year's Eve party

Balagan: Hebrew for 'craziness'. Can be used to describe anything from a mess in the kitchen to a wild party.

Sephardic: The Jews of Spain who spread out to North Africa, Southern Europe and the Middle East.

Tétouan: A city in Northern Morocco that sits on the Mediterranean. It is extremely close to Spain (only an hour and a half ferry ride), so during the Spanish Inquisition, thousands of Jews went to live there. That's why Dana and her family speak Spanish!

Jacob's maternal family has lived in Cleveland for several generations. Every Sunday you'll find them at the deli eating a brunch of lox and bagels. Jacob's great-grandmother, Mimi Charlotte (z"l), would order a pickled tongue sandwich and slather it with coleslaw until the ripe age of 96. Mimi would make gefilte fish from scratch for her 100-person family. In the kitchen, she would say things like, "Double the salt, then mix it until it looks right," or "Don't forget to put the peels of the onion in the gefilte fish. It adds color!"

Jacob's great-grandmother Mimi Charlotte (z"l)

Although Jacob was raised with Ashkenazi* customs, his father's family traces back to Sephardic Greek Jewry. At our wedding, Jacob's grandpa, Albert, started speaking in Ladino* with Dana's family (we had never heard him speak this language before). Also, his grandma, Rolene, told us that they had a Henna Party*, which is an important Sephardic tradition. We guess that's where Jacob's love of Sephardic food (and woman) comes from!

Ashkenazi: The Jews of Central and Eastern Europe.

Ladino: The Judeo-Spanish language that unified Sephardic Jewry throughout the diaspora. It is a combination of Medieval Spanish, Portuguese, Hebrew and Arabic.

Henna Party: A pre-wedding celebration during which henna ink is smudged on the palms of the bride, groom and the guests for good-luck. This is a tradition that has been in Dana's family for generations. It was a complete surprise that Jacob's grandparents did this too!

Jacob:

The first time I met Dana's family was at her parent's house in Jerusalem. It was at Shabbat dinner, and I was lucky enough to sit next to Safta Rachel, Dana's maternal grandmother, who was born in Urfa*, Turkey. Safta is as sharp as a Turkish kebab skewer and very outspoken, to say the least. I could feel her eyeing me up and down, thinking, "Who is this skinny American boy Dana brought home?" Wait no, she said it out loud! Before diving into my soup, I stirred in a spoonful of schug*, a trick I acquired after living in Israel for a few years. Safta couldn't have been more impressed by my love of spicy food (good move, Jacob) and by the end of the dinner, Safta was asking when I planned to propose.

Jerusalem, 2013
Purim

Dana:

The first time I met Jacob's family was at his house in Cleveland, Ohio. Jacob's mom, Cindy, can throw together a five-course meal in the time it takes you to open the fridge and decide what you're in the mood for. During that trip, I tasted Sweet Noodle Kugel for the first time, made by Jacob's grandmother Mimi Linda. Although it seemed weird to have a dessert as a main course, it was amazing to celebrate Shabbat with flavors that were completely new to me.

Urfa: Dana's maternal grandmother was born in Urfa, a city in southeastern Turkey near the Syrian border. Urfa is believed to be the hometown of Abraham, a forefather of Judaism. Urfa is also known for the Urfa Pepper, a hot chili with a smoky taste. Abraham probably had an affinity for spicy food.

Schug: A fiery Yemenite condiment made from chili peppers, garlic, cilantro and lemon. Since about 450,000 Yemenite Jews live in Israel, schug has become a staple of Israeli cuisine. Only about 50 Jews remain in Yemen.

Moroccan Fish & Matzo Ball Soup

In our home, we've combined the best of both worlds. During Shabbat dinner, freshly baked challah is ripped apart, sprinkled with salt and passed around. Dips are everywhere: hummus, baba ghanoush and salty tahina. The first course is spicy Moroccan fish in a lemony tomato sauce, Dana's grandmother's recipe. Next is chicken soup with baseball-sized, fluffy matzo balls. This is also grandma's recipe, but from Jacob's side of the family. At our Shabbat table, Jewish dishes from all over the world sit together.

This culture mashup happens at other Shabbat tables too, especially in Israel. There, you'll find the most colorful assortment of cuisines in every household and on every street block. Ethiopian restaurants serve flat, green, bubbly bread topped with a variety of stews. The Iraqi restaurant next to it serves different types of kibbeh (fried bulgur stuffed with minced lamb), served in beet soup or with a side of tahini. Right across the street from those two restaurants sits an American-style bagel café selling lox, shmear and the works. When you're walking down the street in Jerusalem and need to decide between Ethiopian, Iraqi or American cuisine, you get the feeling that Jewish food is much more diverse than you ever imagined.

Tel Aviv, 2016
Israeli breakfast for the win

One day, as we were splitting an Israeli breakfast at a café in Tel Aviv, we marvelled at the incredibly unique and delicious food that was right at our doorstep. That's when we came up with the idea for Jewlish, a video channel that highlights the mouth-watering dishes that Jewish food has to offer. We were immediately excited by the idea, but where to start? We may have been passionate about food, but we had little knowledge of videography or production.

The evolution of our film studio

Since this isn't the place for a lesson on video production, we'll just tell you about a few of the ridiculous things that happened in our film studio (if you could even call it that). Some of the problems we faced lead to cuts, burns and flying food.

At the time, we lived in Tel Aviv next to the bustling Carmel Market. The selection of seasonal fruits and vegetables were on another level and we would cook something different and inventive every day. One day, Jacob came home with fresh sea bream wrapped in paper. One of us stood on our dining room table with a camera pointing downwards while the other stuffed lemon slices and fresh parsley into the fish. After crisping up under the broiler, the sea bream was perfect. The video on the other hand, looked like it was filmed during an earthquake.

We eventually learned that there are four essential components to filming a good video:

- Lights
- Camera
- Something to hold it all up
- Editing software

If the first phase of the film studio is called the 'table standing phase', the second can be called the 'chair phase'. We could try to explain the chair phase, however, only a picture would do it justice. Yes, this was our fancy film studio.

This hilarious chair contraption not only cast a shadow across the video background, but also wobbled when anything touched it. If we were serious about making videos, we needed some legit equipment.

Instead of buying expensive video equipment, we decided to make it ourselves! Our neighbors were renovating their apartment, so we asked their construction team to cut our Ikea cabinet into planks.

This camera rig was called 'The Beast' since it took up our entire kitchen and living room. It took 30 minutes to set up and take down every time we filmed a video. You can see that the lights were wrapped in wax paper and taped onto the frame. Although The Beast was undeniably a fire hazard, it survived for 5 months and didn't burn down our building. Jacob did get electrocuted once or twice, but the pain was worth it since The Beast helped us realize that Jewlish was more than a farfetched dream.

In order to grow Jewlish to its full potential, we decided to move to Los Angeles, the heart of the entertainment world. However, before we moved away, The Beast caused a dramatic scene. On our last day of filming in Israel, Jacob tripped over a loose wire. In one of those slow-motion 'uh oh' moments, The Beast tipped over and splintered into pieces. It was probably upset that we were leaving.

Now, in LA, we have a real studio – one that isn't a fire hazard. The videos look more beautiful than ever. It's incredible to see how Jewlish has grown from a chair on a table to a published cookbook. Thanks to our followers and the world's love of Jewish food, our dream has become a reality.

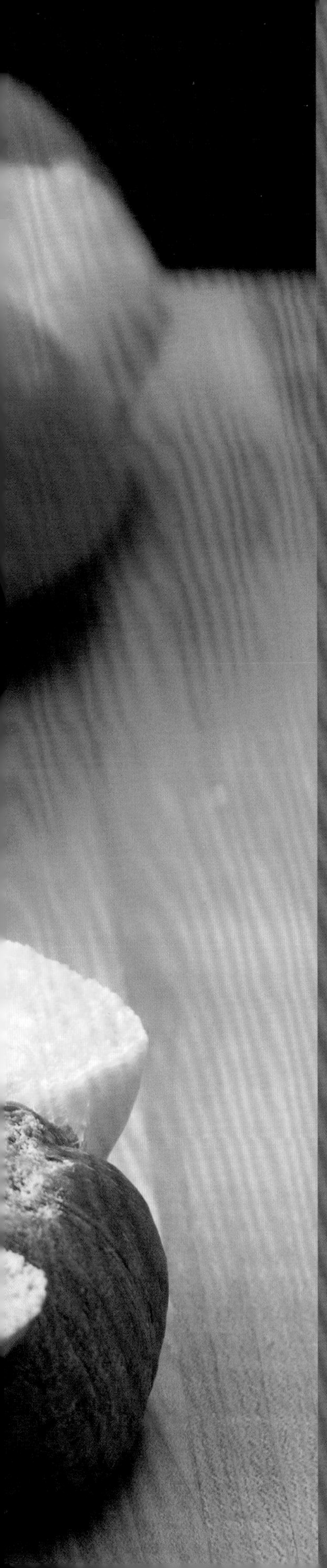

CHALLAH

חַלָּה

['Hallah' - with a hard h]

BRAIDING A 6 STRAND CHALLAH

BRAIDING A 2 STRAND CHALLAH

ZAHTAR & OLIVE STUFFED CHALLAH

CHALLAH IN A BAG

PRETZEL CHALLAH

GARLIC STUFFED CHALLAH KNOTS

CINNAMON ROLL CHALLAH

HONEY WHOLE WHEAT CHALLAH

APPLE CHALLAH

how to braid a 6 STRAND CHALLAH

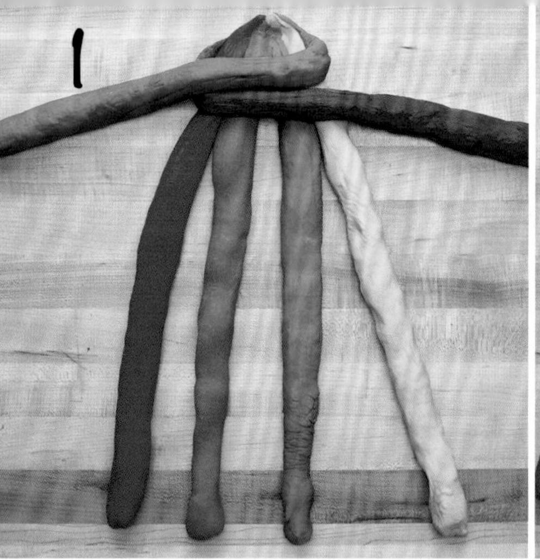

Cross the left and right strands.

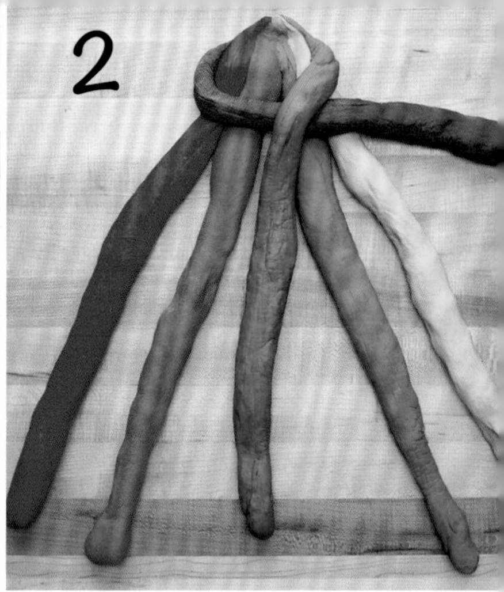

Top left into the middle.

Second from right goes over.

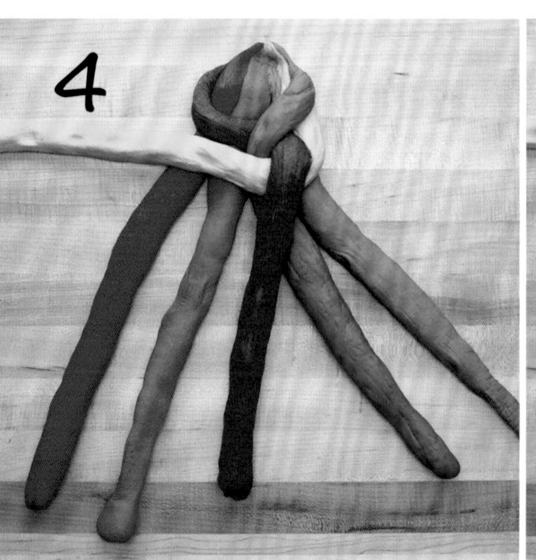

Top right into the middle.

Second from left goes over.

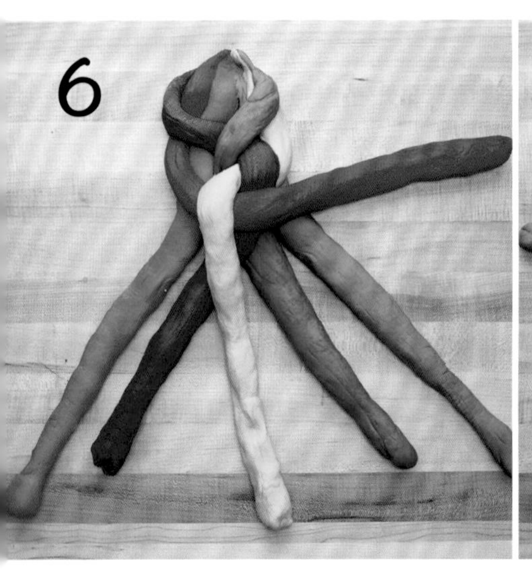

Top left into the middle.

Second from right goes over.

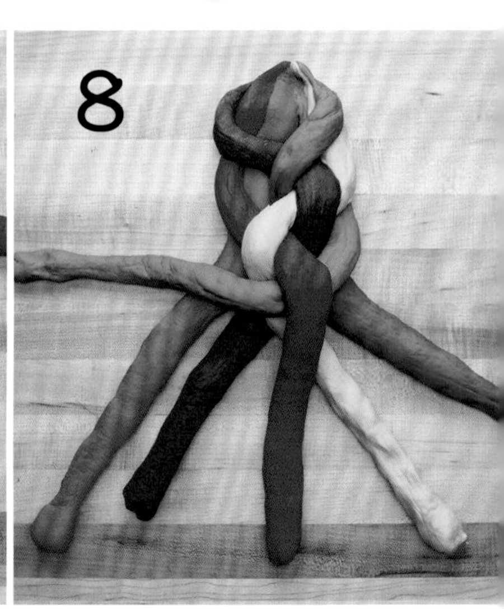

Top right into the middle.

Repeat steps 5 - 8 until you reach the end...

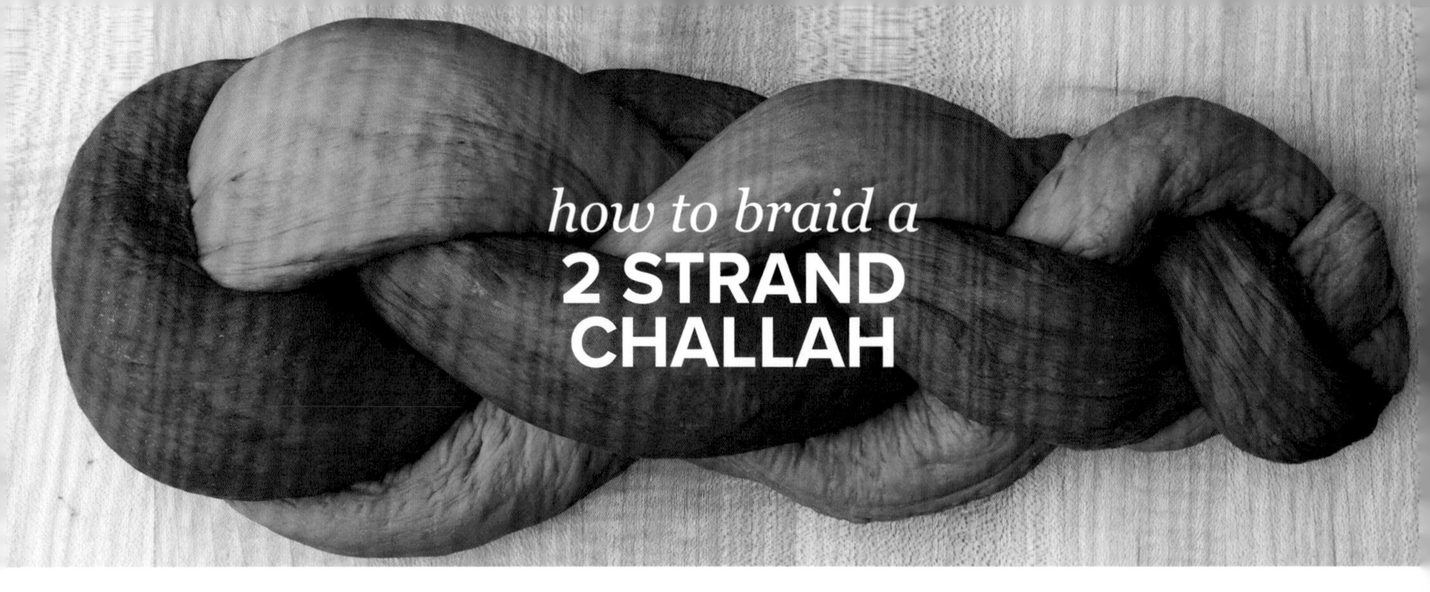

Cross the strands.

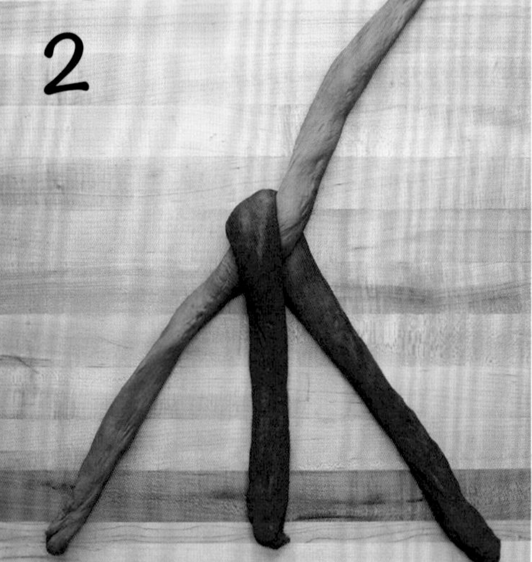

Top left into the middle.

Second from right goes over.

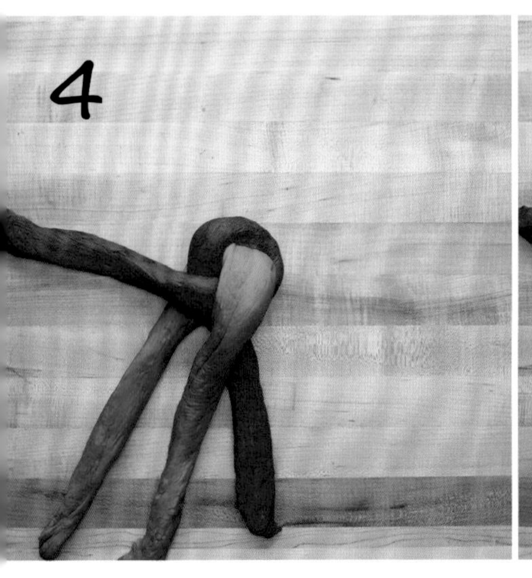

Top right into the middle.

Second from left goes over.

Top left into the middle.

Repeat steps 3 - 6 until you reach the end...

Second from right goes over.

Top right into the middle.

Second from left goes over.

Top left into the middle.

Second from right goes over.

Pinch the ends together.

Zahtar & Olive Stuffed Challah

Classy on the outside, party on the inside.

Makes: 1 large challah

DOUGH
¾ cup warm water
2¼ teaspoons active dry yeast (1 packet)
3 tablespoons sugar
2 tablespoons vegetable oil
1 large egg
1 teaspoon salt
3 cups all-purpose flour

FILLING
3 tablespoons olive oil
3 tablespoons za'atar
½ cup sliced olives

TOPPING
1 egg
Za'atar

TIP
For a classic challah recipe, use this recipe without the filling. Simply braid and sprinkle with sesame or poppy seeds instead.

א In a large bowl, use a fork to mix the warm water, yeast, sugar, vegetable oil, egg and salt. Gradually add the flour and mix until a dough forms. When the dough is too dense to mix, use your hands.

ב On a floured surface, knead until the dough becomes soft and smooth, about 5 to 10 minutes. Place the dough in a bowl, cover and rise in a warm part of the kitchen until it doubles in size, at least 1 hour.

ג Separate the dough into 3 even pieces. Use a rolling pin to flatten the first piece of dough into a 9 by 9 inch square. Spread 1 tablespoon of olive oil then sprinkle za'atar and some sliced olives. Roll it up and pinch the ends. Repeat for the other two pieces of dough. Stretch the strands to 12 inches in length. Braid and transfer to a non-stick baking tray.

ד Brush with a beaten egg. Rise in a warm part of the kitchen for 45 minutes. Preheat the oven to 350°F / 175°C.

ה Brush with more egg and sprinkle with za'atar. Bake for 30 minutes. The challah is done when you tap the bottom of the loaf and it makes a hollow sound.

Challah in a Bag

a.k.a. the lazy man's challah. It's easy as aleph, bet, gimmel.

Makes: 1 large challah

DOUGH

2¼ teaspoons active dry yeast (1 packet)
¾ cup warm water
3 tablespoons sugar
1½ teaspoons salt
⅓ cup vegetable oil
3 cups all-purpose flour

TOPPING

1 egg (for vegan challah, substitute olive oil)
Sesame seeds

א In a 1 gallon ziplock bag, add the yeast, water, sugar, salt, oil and flour. Zip it closed.

ב Squeeze the dough in the bag until all the ingredients are evenly mixed, about 5 minutes. Kids are especially good at this step!

ג Fill a large bowl with warm water from the sink. Place the bag in the bowl to rise for 1 hour.

ד Separate the dough into 3 even pieces. On a floured surface, roll them out into strands. If there are any clumps of flour in the dough, knead them out. Braid and transfer to a non-stick baking tray.

ה Preheat oven to 350°F / 175°C. Brush the challah with a beaten egg (or olive oil) and sprinkle with sesame seeds. Let the challah rise for 45 minutes.

ו Brush with egg (or olive oil) again and sprinkle with more sesame seeds. Bake for 25-30 minutes. The challah is done when you tap the bottom of the loaf and it makes a hollow sound.

TIP
You're done squeezing the bag when there are no clumps of flour left in the dough.

Pretzel & Challah – a match made in heaven.

Makes: 2 small challahs

DOUGH

2¼ teaspoons active dry yeast (1 packet)
¾ cup warm water
3 tablespoons sugar
2 tablespoons vegetable oil
1 large egg
1 teaspoon salt
3 cups all-purpose flour

PRETZEL

4 cups boiling water
½ cup baking soda

TOPPING

1 egg
Coarse pretzel salt

TIP

Baking time depends on the size of the challah so if you are making one big challah instead of two small ones, bake it for 18 to 20 minuntes instead.

א In a large bowl, use a fork to mix the yeast, warm water, sugar, oil, egg and salt. Gradually add the flour and mix until a dough forms. When the dough is too dense to mix, use your hands.

ב On a floured surface, knead until the dough becomes soft and smooth, about 5 to 10 minutes. Place the dough in a bowl, cover and rise in a warm part of the kitchen until it doubles in size, at least 1 hour.

ג Place the dough on the counter and cut it in half. Cut each half into 3 even pieces. Roll them out into strands and braid two separate challahs.

ד For this step (we call it 'pretzelfication'), bring 4 cups of water to a boil. Pour it into a large casserole dish. Add the baking soda and mix with a fork until it is completely dissolved.

ה Gently place the challahs into the water for 15 seconds on each side, one challah at a time, using a spatula to carefully flip. Remove the challahs directly onto a baking sheet.

ו Preheat the oven to 375°F / 190°C. Let the challahs rise for 30 minutes.

ז Brush with a beaten egg and sprinkle generously with coarse pretzel salt. Bake for 15 minutes. The challah is done when you tap the bottom of the loaf and it makes a hollow sound.

Pretzel Challah

Makes: 10 challah knots

DOUGH

1 large egg

⅓ cup olive oil

1¾ cups warm water

4½ teaspoons active dry yeast (2 packets)

⅓ cup sugar

1 tablespoon salt

7 cups all-purpose flour

FILLING

⅓ cup olive oil

1 head garlic, peeled and sliced

Parsley flakes

TOPPING

1 egg

4 cloves garlic, chopped

Parsley flakes

Kosher salt

א In a large bowl, use a fork to mix the egg, oil, water, yeast, sugar and salt. Gradually add the flour and mix until a dough forms. When the dough is too dense to mix, use your hands.

ב On a floured surface, knead until the dough becomes soft and smooth, about 5 to 10 minutes. Place the dough in a bowl, cover and rise in a warm part of the kitchen until it doubles in size, at least 1 hour.

ג Meanwhile, cook the olive oil and sliced garlic over medium-low heat until lightly golden, about 4 minutes. Set aside.

ד Split the dough into 10 evenly-sized pieces. Use a rolling pin to flatten each piece of dough into a square. Spread a spoonful of oil and garlic on the dough. Roll it up into a strand and pinch the ends. Stretch with your hands then twist into a simple knot. It's okay if this gets messy!

ה Place the rolls on a baking tray and cover with a towel. Let them rise for 30 minutes. Preheat the oven to 425°F / 220°C.

ו Brush the rolls with a beaten egg and sprinkle the chopped garlic, parsley and salt. Bake for 15 minutes. The rolls are done when you tap the bottom of a loaf and it makes a hollow sound.

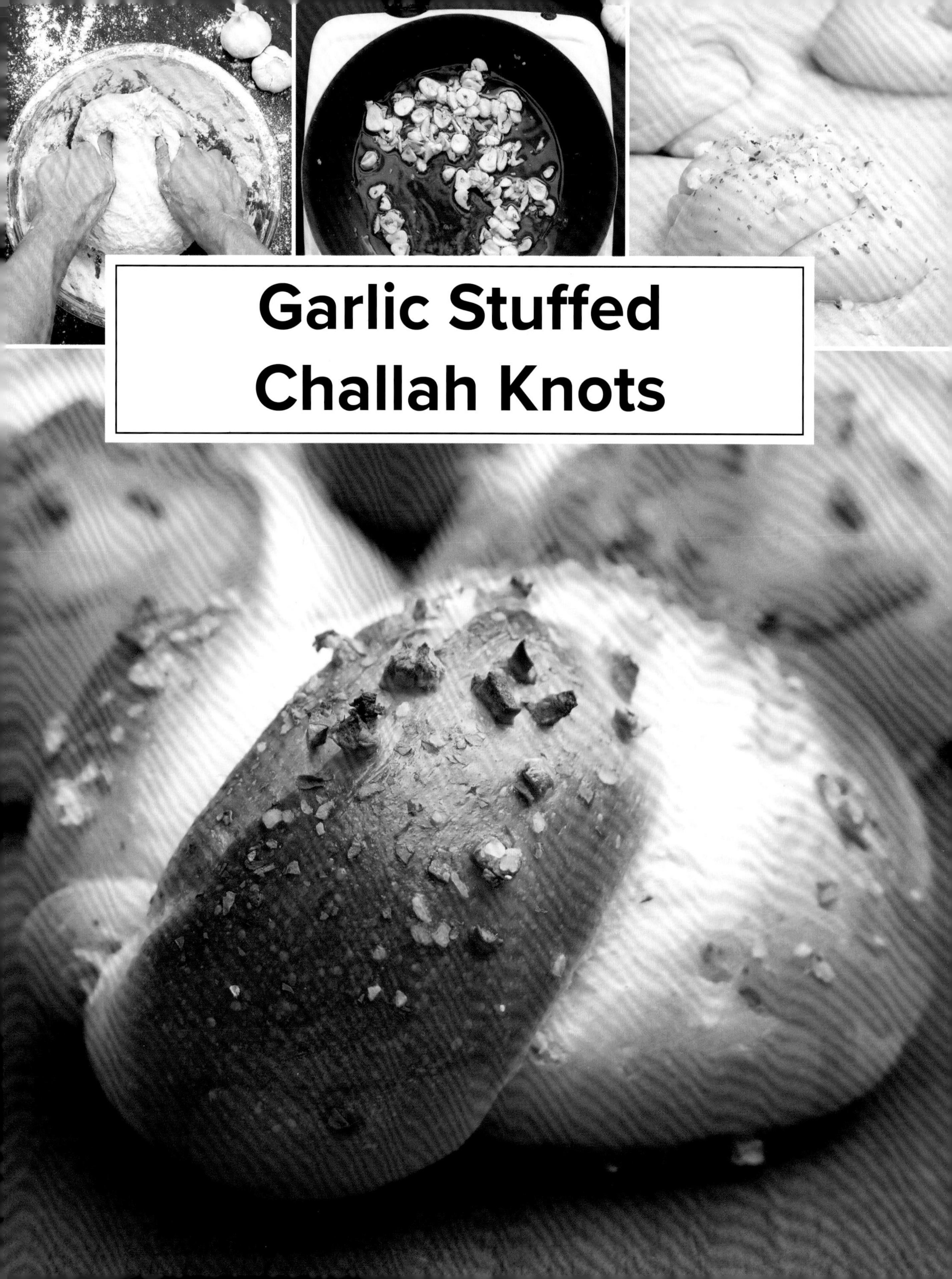

Garlic Stuffed Challah Knots

Cinnamon Roll Challah

Let's get rollin'.

Makes: 1 large challah

DOUGH

3½ cups all-purpose flour

2 large eggs

2¼ teaspoons active dry yeast (1 packet)

3 tablespoons honey

⅓ cup olive oil

1 teaspoon salt

⅔ cup warm water

FILLING

⅓ cup canola oil

¾ cup brown sugar

1½ teaspoons cinnamon

⅛ teaspoon salt

TOPPING

1 egg

Coarse sugar, optional

TIP

You can use a bowl too, but this is way more fun!

א Place the flour in the center of a large surface. Make a 'bowl' in the middle of the flour like a crater in the top of a pyramid (see photo).

ב In the 'bowl' add the eggs, yeast, honey, oil, salt and half of the water. Mix with a fork. Use your hands to drag in some of the flour from the edges into the center. Add the other half of the water while there is still a bowl shape. Mix into a dough and knead for 5 to 10 minutes until smooth.

ג Cover with a towel and rise until the dough has doubled in size, at least 1 hour.

ד While the dough is rising, make the filling. In a small bowl, mix together the oil, brown sugar, cinnamon and salt.

ה Separate the dough into 3 even pieces. Use a rolling pin to flatten the first piece of dough into a 9 by 9 inch square. Spread 1/3 of the cinnamon mixture on top, leaving 1 inch of space around the edges. Roll it up and pinch the ends. Repeat for the other two pieces of dough. Stretch each strand to 12 inches in length. Braid and transfer to a non-stick baking tray.

ו Brush with a beaten egg. Let it rise for 45 minutes in a warm part of the kitchen. Preheat the oven to 375°F / 190°C.

ז Gently brush again with egg and sprinkle with coarse sugar. Bake for 30 minutes. If the challah is getting too dark, place a piece of aluminum foil on top. The challah is done when you tap the bottom of the loaf and it makes a hollow sound.

שבת

Honey Whole Wheat Challah

So healthy – you can eat the 'whole' thing.

Makes: 1 large challah

DOUGH

1 cup warm water
2¼ teaspoons active dry yeast (1 packet)
⅓ cup honey
1 large egg
¼ cup olive oil
1 teaspoon salt
3½ cups of whole wheat flour

TOPPING

1 egg
Seeds (pumpkin, sesame, poppy)

א In a large bowl, use a fork to mix the warm water, yeast, honey, egg, oil and salt. Gradually add the flour and mix until a dough forms. When the dough is too dense to mix, use your hands.

ב On a floured surface, knead until the dough becomes soft and smooth, about 5 to 10 minutes. Place the dough in a bowl, cover and rise in a warm part of the kitchen until it doubles in size, at least 1 hour.

ג Separate the dough into 3 even pieces and roll them out into strands. Braid and transfer to a non-stick baking tray.

ד Cover with a towel and allow the challah to rise until it looks light and airy, about 1 hour. Preheat oven to 350°F / 175°C.

ה Brush with a beaten egg and sprinkle with seeds. Bake for 30 minutes. The challah is done when you tap the bottom of the loaf and it makes a hollow sound.

Apple Challah

Originally a top-secret recipe by Cindy, Jacob's mom. Now tried and tested by thousands of Jewlish fans.

Makes: 1 large challah

DOUGH

2¼ teaspoons active dry yeast (1 packet)
1 cup warm water
⅓ cup sugar
2 large eggs
1¼ teaspoons salt
⅓ cup vegetable oil
⅛ teaspoon sesame oil
3¾ cups all-purpose flour + ¼ more for dusting

FILLING

1 large granny smith apple, thinly sliced
3 tablespoons sugar
1 teaspoon ground cinnamon

TOPPING

1 egg
Coarse sugar

א In a large bowl, use a fork to mix the yeast, warm water, sugar, eggs, salt, vegetable oil and sesame oil. Gradually add the flour and mix until a dough forms. When the dough is too dense to mix, use your hands.

ב Transfer the dough to a floured surface and knead for 5 minutes - it should be a little sticky. Place the dough in a bowl, cover and rise in a warm part of the kitchen until it doubles in size, at least 1 hour.

ג On a floured surface, roll out the dough into a rectangle about 10 inches wide and 14 inches long. Trim the edges to shape it into a rectangle.

ד Place a line of apple slices ⅓ of the way from the bottom of the rectangle (see photo). There should be enough space below the apples to fold the dough over them. Sprinkle 1 tablespoon of sugar and ⅓ teaspoon of cinnamon over the apples. Fold the dough over and repeat two more times. There may only be enough space for 2 rows of apples, and that's okay. If there is any extra dough at the top, fold it over the rest of the roll.

ה Cut the roll into 8 sections. Place each section in a greased bundt pan long-ways (see photo). Place an apple slice between each section. Brush with a beaten egg and sprinkle with coarse sugar.

ו Let the challah rest for 1 hour. Preheat oven to 350°F / 175°C. Bake for 30-35 minutes until golden.

DIPS

מִמְרָח
[Mimrah] - literally translates to 'spread'

BABA GANOUSH

HUMMUS

TAHINI WITH MINT

MATBUCHA

VEGETARIAN CHOPPED LIVER

Baba Ganoush

In Israel, 'baba' is often called salat hazilim (eggplant salad) or hazilim b'tchina (eggplant in tahini). In Arabic, baba ganoush translates to 'pampered daddy'.

This mezze dip is best when it is very smoky, a characteristic that doesn't come with the store-bought variety. Take care to wrap the eggplants well, so you can blast them with fire without making a mess. Some eggplants have slightly bitter seeds, so taste them after you peel off the burnt eggplant skin. Sometimes they're delicious and should be included. Also, while garlic is traditionally included in baba, this recipe is great without since it's already so smoky and flavorful.

Serves 6

2 medium-sized eggplants
½ cup of raw tahini
1 tablespoon lemon juice
2 cloves crushed garlic (optional)
¼ teaspoon salt

א With a fork, prick a couple holes in the eggplants. Wrap each eggplant in two layers of aluminum foil. Place them directly on a stovetop flame on medium heat for about 20 minutes, rotating every 5 minutes, until they smell very smoky. Or, you can use a grill and skip the foil.

ב Allow the eggplants to cool.

ג Over the sink, unwrap the foil and place the eggplants in a strainer. Peel off the skin with your hands and cut them in half. Some liquid will drain out into the sink. Remove the seeds (optional - sometimes eggplant seeds taste bitter).

ד Place the eggplants in a bowl. Add raw tahini, lemon juice, garlic and salt.

ה Mash with a fork. If it's too liquidy, add more raw tahini. Taste and adjust lemon and salt to your preference.

Hummus

Serves 8

2 cups dried chickpeas
1 teaspoon baking soda
1 onion, peeled
⅔ cup raw tahini
⅓ cup lemon juice, about 2 large lemons
2 cloves garlic, crushed
2 teaspoons salt

TOPPINGS
Olive oil
Paprika
Boiled egg, quartered
Chopped parsley
1 onion, quartered

א Place the chickpeas in a large bowl with ½ teaspoon of baking soda. Cover the chickpeas with cold water and soak overnight (at least 8 hours).

ב Drain the chickpeas, rinse and place in a large pot. Cover with water that goes 2 inches over the chickpeas. Add ½ teaspoon of baking soda along with the peeled onion.

ג Cover and cook on medium heat until the chickpeas are soft enough to easily smush between two fingers. This takes about an hour and a half.

ד Strain the chickpeas and transfer to a blender or food processor. Set some chickpeas aside for garnishing. You can add the onion to the food processor too.

ה Add the tahini, lemon juice, garlic, 2 tablespoons of water and salt. Blend. You may need to scrape down the sides. Add more water, one tablespoon at a time, until it reaches a smooth and creamy consistency. Note that warm hummus will thicken as it cools. Adjust salt to taste.

TIP 1: Small chickpeas make smoother, tastier hummus.
TIP 2: Use Israeli tahini if possible - a high quality tahini makes a silky-smooth hummus.
PRO-TIP: Save the liquid from the chickpeas to use as a soup stock.

Tahini with Mint

This dip is delicious with everything. Dipping bread, dressing salad or with fish. Tahini is a lifestyle.

Serves 6

1 cup mint leaves (bitter stems removed)
½ cup raw tahini
2 tablespoons lemon juice (half a lemon)
½ teaspoon salt
6 tablespoons water
1 clove garlic, peeled

א Add all the ingredients to a blender or food processor.

ב Blend until it reaches a smooth consistency.

ג Adjust salt to taste.

TIP
Shake and mix your jar of raw tahini before using. The oil tends to rise to the top and the sesame sinks to the bottom.

1/2 tsp/2.5ml

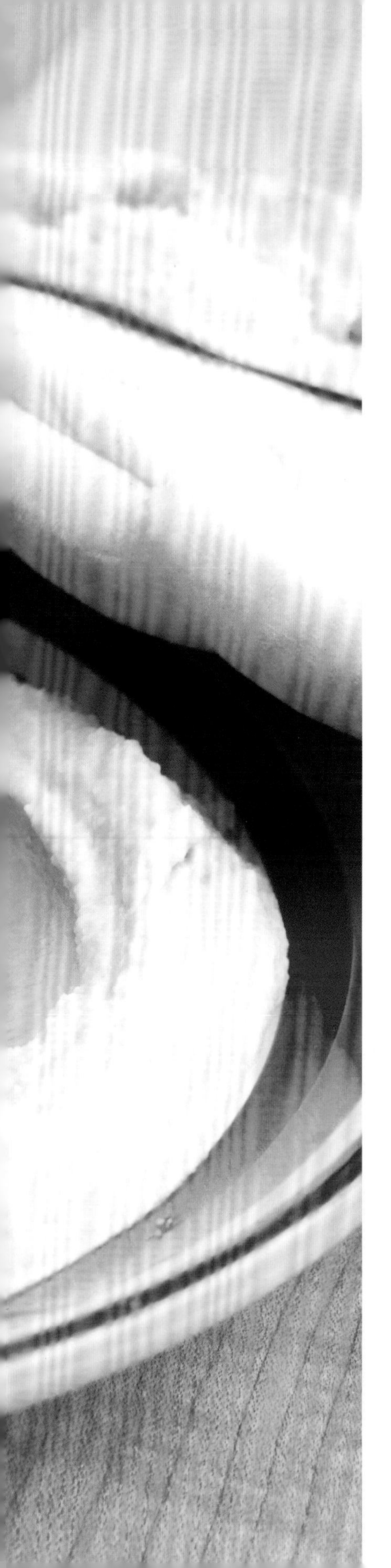

Matbucha

Serves 6

2 red bell peppers
1 chili pepper, if you like the heat
2 cans peeled diced tomatoes, 14.5 oz (410 g) each
5 cloves garlic, sliced
1 tablespoon sugar
4 tablespoons olive oil
1 teaspoon salt
1 tablespoon paprika

א Place the chili and bell peppers on a baking sheet in the oven. Broil for 20 minutes, flipping after 10. The peppers should be blackened on all sides. Once cool, remove the blackened skin from the peppers. Cut each pepper in half and remove the seeds and stems, or keep some seeds for a spicier dish. Cut the peppers into strips and set aside.

ב While the peppers are in the oven, add the canned tomatoes, sliced garlic and sugar to a pot. Cook on medium heat, stirring occasionally, until it reaches a jam-like consistency, about 20 minutes.

ג Add the olive oil and sliced peppers to the pot. Cook on medium-low heat for 1 hour, stirring occasionally to prevent it from sticking to the bottom of the pan.

ד Add the salt and paprika. Stir and allow to cool before serving.

TIP
Prepare 1 day in advance. Matbucha tastes even better after 1-2 days in the fridge.

Vegetarian Chopped Liver

Serves 8

1 cup whole walnuts
4 tablespoons vegetable oil
2 onions, chopped
1 cup chopped mushrooms, 10 oz (280 g)
4 large eggs, boiled
3 sprigs of parsley
½ teaspoon salt
¼ teaspoon ground black pepper

א Toast the walnuts in a frying pan on medium heat for 2 minutes, stirring often. Remove the walnuts and set aside.

ב Add 2 tablespoons of the oil to the pan and fry the onions on medium-low heat until golden and caramelized, about 20 minutes.

ג Meanwhile, add 2 tablespoons of oil to a second frying pan and cook the mushrooms on medium heat until soft, about 10 minutes.

ד Add the toasted walnuts to a food processor and grind to a powder. Then, add the onions, mushrooms, boiled eggs, walnuts, parsley, salt and pepper. Pulse to your desired consistency. Taste and adjust salt if necessary.

ה Garnish with chopped parsley, chopped hard-boiled egg and sliced red onion.

VEGETABLES

יְרָקוֹת

[Ye-ra-kote] - similar to the Hebrew word for green, 'yarok'

Mediterranean Ptitim Salad

In the 1950s, only a few years after the state of Israel was established, the Israeli population had doubled, and food was in short supply. So they did what Israelis do best – invent something new. As a cheap wheat-based substitute for rice, ptitim was born! Ptitim has come a long way since then, making appearances in upscale restaurants. Internationally, it is now known as 'Israeli couscous' or 'pearl couscous'.

Serves 6

1½ cups ptitim
1 teaspoon olive oil
½ teaspoon cumin
1¾ cups water
1 cup cherry tomatoes, halved
½ cup mint, chopped
½ cup parsley, chopped
½ red onion, chopped
2 pickled artichoke hearts, quartered
Goat feta, crumbled

TOPPING

Juice of ½ lemon
1 tablespoon olive oil
½ teaspoon date honey (known as 'silan' in Hebrew, or substitute regular honey)
Salt and pepper, to taste

א Add ptitim to a pot on medium heat with the olive oil and cumin. Stir and cook for 1 minute. Add the water, bring to a boil and cover on low heat for 12 minutes.

ב Wait a few minutes for the ptitim to cool then add them to your salad bowl with the tomatoes, mint, parsley, red onion, artichoke hearts and feta.

ג Mix the lemon juice, olive oil, date honey, salt and pepper in a small bowl. Pour over the salad. It doesn't need much salt because of the feta cheese.

ד Toss gently and serve at room temperature.

Cauliflower-Rice Tabbouleh Salad

Originating in the mountain range between Syria and Lebanon, tabbouleh is now popular in Israel and throughout the Middle East. This version uses cauliflower rice, which has become super 'duper' trendy, and is a delicious gluten-free substitution for the bulgur wheat. Serve this on a hot day along with hummus, baba ganoush and bread for dipping. Jewish families in Syria used to serve tabbouleh salad with romaine leaves for scooping it up.

Serves 4

½ small cauliflower
2 cups flat-leaf parsley, finely chopped
½ cup mint leaves, finely chopped
1 small cucumber, chopped
1 cup cherry tomatoes, chopped
½ onion, finely chopped
¼ cup extra-virgin olive oil
3 tablespoons lemon juice
½ teaspoon salt
¼ teaspoon black pepper
¼ teaspoon cumin
Pomegranate seeds (optional)

CAULIFLOWER RICE:

א Cut the cauliflower in half, cut out the core, and cut into chunks.

ב Place the cauliflower into a food processor. Pulse about 5 times or until pieces are the size of rice grains. You can also use a hand grater for this step.

ג Transfer the cauliflower rice to a microwavable bowl. Microwave for 2½ minutes.

TABBOULEH SALAD:

ד Literally just add everything to a bowl and mix.

TIP 1: It's all about the parsley. Fresh parsley is traditionally the main ingredient in tabbouleh salad.

TIP 2: Make sure the parsley and mint are dry before adding them to the salad. Extra water in the salad dilutes the flavor.

Couscous Salad with Pomegranate Chicken

Serves 4

CHICKEN

2 chicken breasts, cubed

1 tablespoon harissa paste

¼ cup pomegranate juice

1 tablespoon olive oil

SALAD

1 cup couscous

1 cup boiling water

½ teaspoon salt

1 cup cherry tomatoes, chopped

½ cup mint, chopped

½ cup parsley, chopped

2 tablespoons pomegranate seeds

DRESSING

1 tablespoons lemon juice

3 tablespoons extra-virgin olive oil

Salt and pepper

א Place the cubed chicken in a bowl with the harissa paste and pomegranate juice. Mix, cover with plastic wrap and marinate for 15 minutes.

ב Add 1 cup of couscous to a large bowl with 1 cup of boiling water and ½ teaspoon of salt. Stir and cover for 10 minutes. Meanwhile, chop your vegetables. When the 10 minutes are up, fluff the couscous with a fork.

ג Place a pan on medium-high heat. Once hot, add 1 tablespoon of olive oil and add the marinated chicken. Cook for 6 to 8 minutes until cooked through.

ד To serve, place the chicken on top of the couscous along with the cherry tomatoes, mint, parsley, cilantro and pomegranate seeds.

ה Mix the dressing ingredients in a separate bowl and pour over the salad. Sprinkle additional salt and pepper to taste.

TIP

For a vegan option, substitute the chicken with toasted cashews and pistachios.

Spicy North African Carrot Salad

You're sitting at a restaurant on the Tel Aviv docks next to the gentle waves of the Mediterranean. You're surrounded by white tablecloths, white wine and whole roasted fish on platters. The waiters place ten different salads on the table. This is one of those salads. How did this North African salad find its way to a Tel Aviv fish restaurant? Well, that's Israel in a nutshell.

Serves 6

7 medium sized carrots
4 tablespoons olive oil
4 cloves garlic
1 teaspoon cumin
2 teaspoons paprika
Pinch of cayenne pepper
¼ teaspoon salt
1 tablespoon lemon juice
¼ cup chopped parsley or cilantro leaves

א Peel carrots and cut into ¼ inch cylinders.

ב Add carrots to a pot and cover with water. Bring to a boil and cook for 10 minutes until tender but still crisp. Strain carrots and transfer to a bowl.

ג Add olive oil to a pan on medium-low heat. Add the chopped garlic, cumin, paprika and cayenne pepper. Cook for 1 minute, stirring often. Be careful not to burn the spices.

ד Pour the mixture on top of the carrots.

ה Add the lemon juice, chopped parsley (or cilantro) and salt. Mix, taste and adjust the salt if necessary.

MEDIUM

Sabich

Fried eggplant and hard-boiled eggs in a pita. This Jewish-Iraqi dish that was originally eaten on Shabbat mornings has become a staple of Israeli street food. Some claim that the word sabich comes from the Arabic word 'sabah', which translates to 'morning'. The most traditional condiment that accompanies sabich is called 'amba', a pickled mango sauce, which can be found in Middle Eastern and some Kosher markets.

Serves 5

5 pitas
1 medium eggplant
1 tablespoon salt
oil, for frying

SIDES
2 potatoes, peeled and sliced to ¼ inch thickness
3 eggs, hard-boiled and sliced
1 bunch parsley, finely chopped
¼ red cabbage, shredded
Tahini
Salt and pepper
Amba (mango sauce)
Schug (spicy chili paste)
Sliced pickles

א Cut the eggplant into half-inch slices. Place the slices on a tray. Sprinkle the eggplant with salt on both sides. Wait 20 minutes for the salt to pull the water out of the eggplant which makes it soft. Wipe off the salt and water with a paper towel.

ב Meanwhile, bring a large pot of water to a boil. Peel and slice the potatoes. Add them to the boiling water, cover and cook for 11 minutes. This is also a good time to prepare the hard boiled eggs.

ג Add enough oil to a frying pan to cover the bottom of the pan, then bring to medium-low heat. Add the eggplant and cook on each side for 4 to 5 minutes. If the flame is too high, the eggplant will burn without cooking on the inside.

ד Remove the eggplant from the oil and place on a paper towel lined tray. Place more paper towels on top and squeeze them down with a spoon to remove the oil from the eggplant.

ה Time to stuff the pitas! Get all the sides ready and add one layer at a time. Don't forget a pinch of salt and pepper – it changes everything.

Borscht

Tradition, tradition!

Serves 6-8

2 tablespoons vegetable oil
2 carrots, grated or finely chopped
1 large onion, grated or finely chopped
3 medium beets
2 potatoes, peeled and cubed
10 cups water
2 teaspoons sugar
Salt and pepper
Dill, for garnish
Sour cream, for garnish

א Place a large pot on medium heat and add the oil. Add the carrots and onion. Cook for 10 minutes until soft.

ב Peel the beets under gently running water to prevent your hands from turning red. Cut into small cubes or matchsticks.

ג Add the beets and potatoes to the pot. Fill with 10 cups of water and simmer until the beets are soft, about 20-25 minutes.

ד Season with sugar, salt and pepper. Adjust to taste.

ה Stir a big dollop of sour cream in each bown. Serve with another dollop, along with a sprig of fresh dill. Can be served hot on a winter night or cold on a summer day.

The best pickles are made at home. We recommend using Kirby cucumbers, which are most similar to the ones you'll find in a deli. Persian cucumbers are widely available and also make classic, crunchy pickles.

Makes: 20 pickles

BRINE

1½ cups water

1 cup white vinegar, 5% acidity

FOR EACH JAR

4-5 cucumbers, depending on size

1 tablespoon kosher salt

1 small bunch of fresh dill

1 teaspoon crushed chili peppers

1 bay leaf

2 cloves of garlic, crushed

א Wash the cucumbers then cut off the ends. Slice each cucumber into 4 spears.

ב For the brine, mix together the water and white vinegar.

ג Fill a few jars with the kosher salt, dill, crushed chili peppers, bay leaf and garlic. Add the cucumber spears so they are tightly packed. Pour the brine to the top and close the jars. You don't need glass jars. Any container will work.

ד Shake to mix the ingredients then place in the fridge.

ה You can eat the pickles after 8 hours, but they are best after several days. They will keep for several weeks.

Dill Pickles

Gadi's Israeli Pickles

Dana's uncle, Gadi, lives next to the Mahane Yehuda market in Jerusalem. One time, he took us to the back streets of the market to show us where the locals go to buy the 'good stuff'. And, by 'good stuff', we're referring to the highest quality produce for the lowest price.

Serves 6-8

VEGETABLES

2 carrots
1 red pepper
1 kohlrabi
1 spicy pepper
¼ cabbage
¼ small cauliflower

BRINE

5 cups water
1½ cups vinegar
2 lemons
1 tablespoon salt
¼ teaspoon turmeric

א Wash the vegetables and cut them into chunks. "Not too thin, not too thick," as Gadi explains. Place the veggies in clean jars. You don't need the glass kind, any container will work.

ב In a pot, add the water, vinegar, salt and turmeric. Squeeze the juice from the two lemons then add in the peels. Boil for 3 minutes then remove from heat.

ג Wait 10 minutes for the brine to cool down then carefully pour the liquid into the jars.

ד Once the jars cool to room temperature, seal them and place in the fridge. Leave for two days (or a day and a half if you really can't wait).

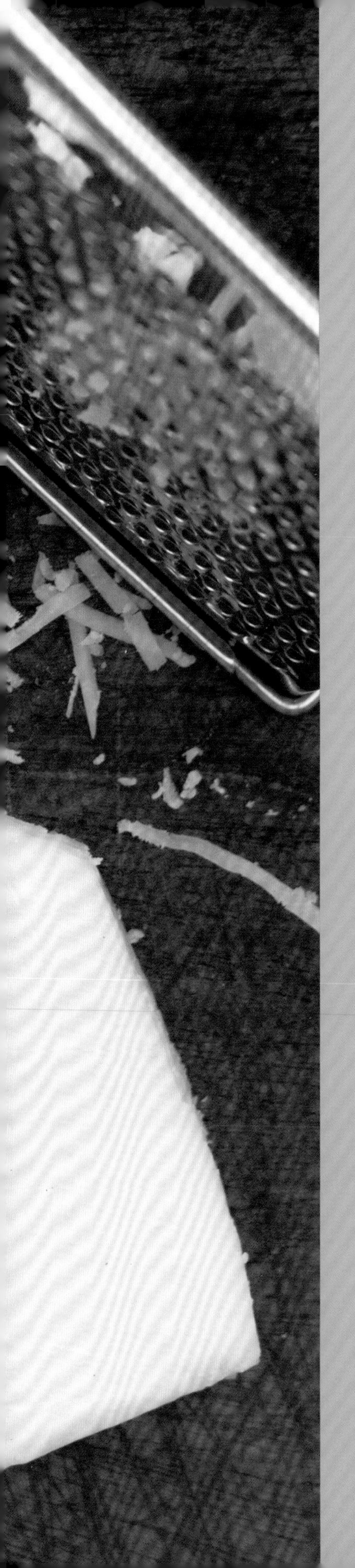

CHEESE

גְבִינָה
[Gvinah]

PITA CHIP PIZZA

BOYOS DE ESPINACA

BEET SHAKSHUKA

CREAMY SPINACH SHAKSHUKA

BOUREKAS 4 WAYS

ONE-POT CHEESY PTITIM

NOODLE KUGEL WITH JAM POKES

Pita Chip Pizza

Easy and cheesy.

Serves 3-4

3 pitas
1 tablespoon olive oil
12 oz (340 g) pizza sauce
10 oz (280 g) shredded mozzarella
3 garlic cloves, sliced
Fresh basil leaves, sliced

א Preheat oven to 375°F / 190°C.

ב Brush the pitas with olive oil on both sides.

ג Stack the pitas and slice 4 times like a pizza, so they are each cut into 8 sections. Spread out on a baking tray. Bake for 20 minutes or until golden brown.

ד Spread your favorite pizza sauce on vthe pita chips, followed by the mozzarella, sliced garlic and basil.

ה Bake for 5 to 10 more minutes untill the cheese is melted.

Boyos de Espinaca

There's nothing like biting into some crispy boyos – through the pastry and into the cheesy filling. This recipe has been passed down among Spanish Jewry for hundreds of years, and with each and every bite, we connect with our past.

The finished boyos freeze well. Simply reheat them in the toaster or in the oven. In the morning, Jacob eats one with his spiced Turkish coffee.

Makes: 12 pastries

DOUGH

1 cup water

1 tablespoon vegetable oil

½ teaspoon salt

3 cups flour

⅓ cup additional oil for the baking pan

FILLING

10 oz (280 g) spinach, chopped

8 oz (225 g) feta, crumbled

4 oz (115 g) Parmesan, shredded

TOPPING

Parmesan, shredded

TIP

Getting the dough thin is tricky, but practice makes perfect! The thinner the dough, the crispier the result. Use a rolling pin to get it started, and continue the stretching by hand.

א Preheat the oven to 400°F / 200°C. Mix the water, 1 tablespoon of oil, salt and flour in a bowl. Knead until a smooth dough forms. If the dough is resisting, let it rest for 30 seconds.

ב Pour ⅓ cup oil onto a baking tray. Pinch off a small ball of dough a little larger than a golf ball. Roll it on the counter to make it smooth. Place it in the oil and flip so it's oiled on all sides. Repeat with all the dough.

ג For the cheese filling, mix the spinach, feta and Parmesan in a bowl.

ד Starting with the balls that were rolled first, take one, flip it in the oil and place it on a smooth surface. With a rolling pin, flatten it into a large rectangle. The dough should be paper thin when stretched to it's full size. If it rips or is too difficult to flatten, let it rest for 15 minutes.

ה Add a row of the spinach mixture to the stretched out dough (see picture). Fold the bottom of the dough over the top, stretching it even thinner along the way. Fold in the sides and roll it up. Coil the roll (see picture) and tuck the end under, so it doesn't uncoil. Place on a non-stick baking tray. Repeat with all the dough.

ו Brush with a beaten egg and sprinkle with shredded Parmesan. Bake until golden brown, about 30 to 40 minutes.

Beet Shakshuka

Serves 1-2

1 tablespoon olive oil
2 cloves garlic
1 chili pepper, minced (optional)
½ beet, grated
½ can diced tomatoes (7 oz / 200 g)
5 tablespoons water
½ teaspoon salt
2 eggs
2 oz (50 g) Feta
Black pepper

א Place a pan on medium heat. Add the oil, garlic, chili pepper and beets. Cook for 5 minutes, stirring occasionally.

ב Turn the heat down to medium-low. Add the diced tomatoes, water and salt. Mix then cover for 20 minutes.

ג Mix again. With a spatula, make a little hole in the sauce and place the eggs. Sprinkle with feta cheese and fresh black pepper. Cover for 3 more minutes then check if eggs are cooked to your preference. Serve with bread for soaking up the sauce.

Creamy Spinach Shakshuka

Shakshuka is originally a Tunisian tomato-based dish. This version, with an Italian twist, has recently popped up in cafés all over Israel.

Serves 1-2

1 teaspoon butter
¼ cup onion, chopped
1 clove garlic, chopped
1 cup baby spinach
½ cup heavy cream
1 teaspoon flour
Salt and pepper
A pinch of nutmeg
2 large eggs
¼ cup mozzarella, shredded

א If using an oven-proof pan, preheat the oven to broil. If not, don't worry, you can still make this. Just skip this step.

ב Place your pan on the stove on medium heat. Add the butter, onion and garlic. Cook for 5 minutes until the onions start to caramelize.

ג Add the spinach, heavy cream, flour, salt, pepper and nutmeg. Mix.

ד Cook until sauce thickens, about 3 minutes. Stir to prevent sticking.

ה With a spatula, make a little hole in the sauce and place the eggs.

ו After the egg is comfortable in its spot, sprinkle the mozzarella.

ז If you're using an oven-proof pan, place it in the oven and broil for 3 minutes for soft yolks or until eggs are cooked to your preference. Otherwise, cover the pan, turn the heat to medium-low and cook for 3 minutes for soft yolks, or until eggs are cooked to your preference. Serve with bread for soaking up the sauce.

OFF

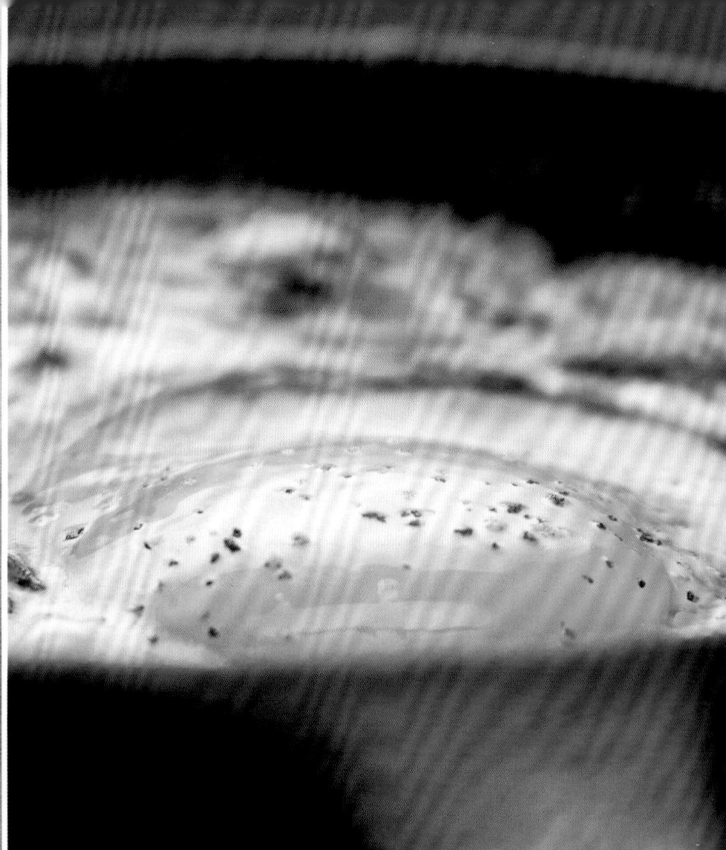

Makes: 18 bourekas

2 sheets puff pastry
2 egg yolks

CLASSIC-CHEESE
1 cup feta cheese, crumbled
1 egg
1 tablespoon flour
Pinch of black pepper

MUSHROOM
1 tablespoon oil
Mushrooms, chopped
Onion, sliced
Salt & pepper

BRIE
Brie cheese

PIZZA
Tomato sauce
Mozzarella, shredded
Sliced olives

TIP
Cold pastry dough is much easier to work with, so work quickly, straight out of the fridge. Or, return it to the fridge if it gets warm.

א Defrost the puff pastry according to the instructions on the package. Trust them. They know what's up when it comes to defrosting dough. Preheat oven to 350°F / 175°C.

ב For the *Classic-Cheese Bourekas*:
Mix the feta, egg, flour and pepper in a bowl.

For the *Mushroom Bourekas*:
Add the oil, onion, mushrooms, salt and pepper to a pan on medium heat. Cook for 15 minutes, stirring occasionally, until soft.

For the *Brie Bourekas*:
Cut the brie into very small pieces.

For the *Pizza Bourekas*:
Get your tomato sauce, mozzarella and sliced olives ready.

ג Once defrosted, flour your baking surface and roll the dough out with a rolling pin into a 12 by 12 inch square. Make sure the dough doesn't stick to the surface.

ד Cut each sheet of dough into 9 squares. Place 1 tablespoon of your favorite filling in the center of each square and fold over into a triangle.

ה Press around the edges with a fork to seal it tightly closed. Brush with egg yolk and sprinkle with sesame seeds.

ו Bake for 30 minutes or until golden brown.

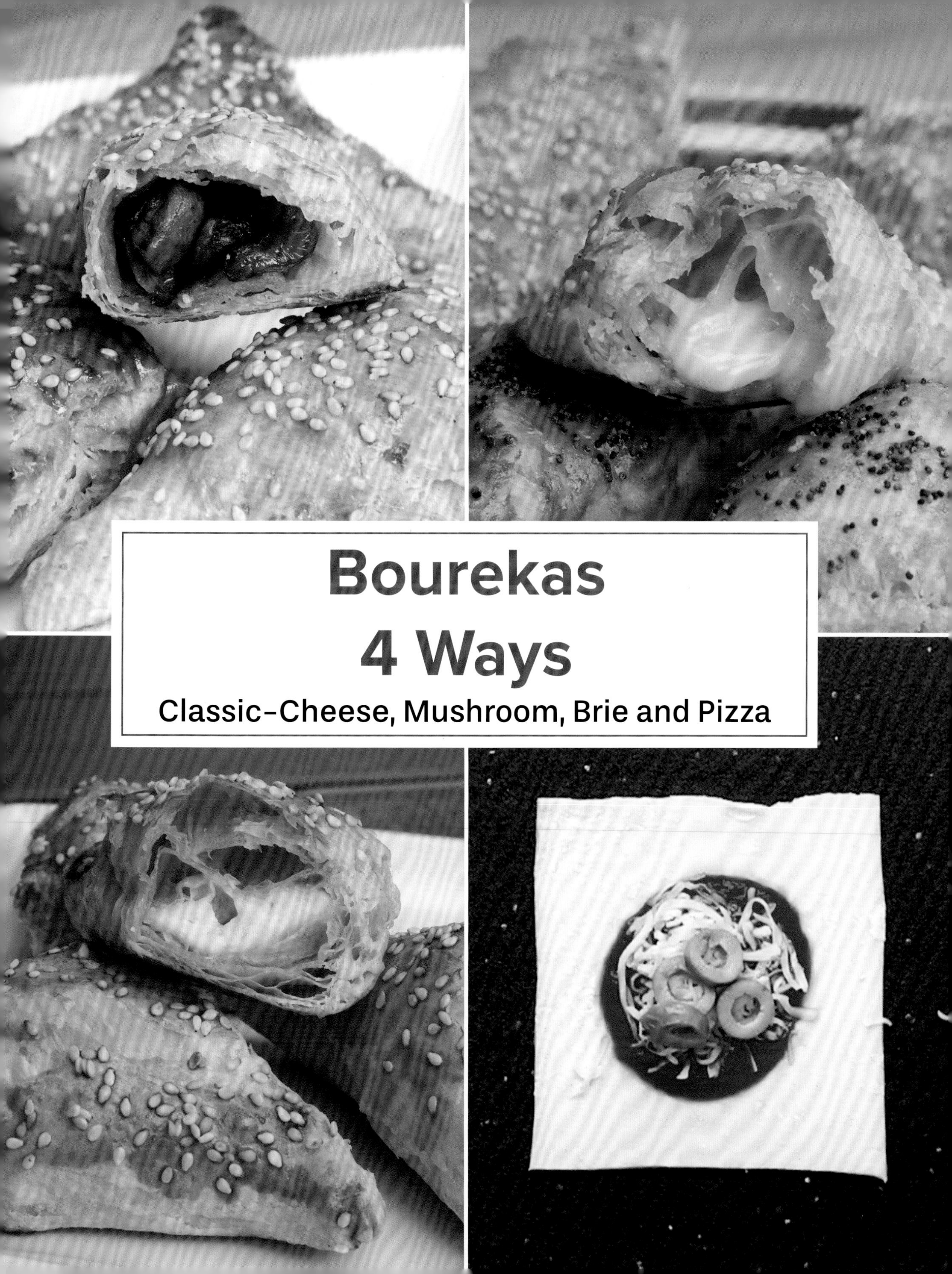

Bourekas 4 Ways

Classic-Cheese, Mushroom, Brie and Pizza

One-Pot Cheesy Ptitim

An Italian-Israeli baby is born.

Serves 6

2 tablespoons butter
¼ cup olive oil
4 cloves garlic, sliced
¼ teaspoon crushed chili peppers
2 cups ptitim
2¼ cups water
1 cup cherry tomatoes, halved
2 cups baby spinach
1 cup Parmesan, shredded + extra for garnish
Salt and pepper
Parsley, for garnish

א Add the butter, olive oil, garlic and crushed chili peppers to a pot on medium heat. Stir and cook for 2 minutes until fragrant.

ב Add the ptitim and stir. Fry the ptitim for 1 to 2 minutes until golden-brown.

ג Add the water and stir. Cover and turn the heat down to medium-low. Simmer for 12 minutes, stirring occasionally.

ד Remove from heat and add the tomatoes, spinach, Parmesan, salt and pepper. Mix.

ה Garnish with chopped parsley and extra Parmesan.

Nutrition
Facts

Noodle Kugel with Jam Pokes

Recipe from Mimi Linda – the queen of kugel. You can prepare this up to a day in advance and bake right before serving.

Serves 6-8

8 oz (225 g) extra-wide egg noodles
3 large eggs
⅓ cup sugar
½ cup butter, melted
8 oz (225 g) cream cheese, at room temperature
16 oz (450 g) cottage cheese
1 teaspoon vanilla
½ cup golden raisins
5 tablespoons blueberry jam
5 tablespoons apricot jam
Cinnamon

א Preheat oven to 350°F / 175°C.

ב Boil egg noodles in water for 5 to 7 minutes until al-dente. Strain.

ג Mix the eggs and sugar in a large bowl.

ד Add the butter, cream cheese, cottage cheese, vanilla and golden raisins. Mix and mash with a fork.

ה Grease an 8 by 8 inch baking dish. Add the strained egg noodles and the egg mixture. Gently mix. It should be quite liquidy.

ו Now we do the 'pokes'. Take a spoon and make a little hole in the kugel. With another spoon, scoop about 1 tablespoon of blueberry or apricot jam into the hole. Repeat about 9 times or until you think the kugel has enough jam. This is a top-secret kugel trick!

ז Dust the top with a thin layer of cinnamon. Bake on a low oven rack for 40 minutes or until the edges are crisped to your liking.

FISH

דָּגִים
[Dag-eem]

HOMEMADE GRAVLAX

PICKLED FISH

HONEY-CARAMELIZED SALMON WITH
APPLE ARUGULA SALAD

SALMON PAELLA

MOROCCAN FISH

Homemade Gravlax

Gravlax is the Scandanavian word for cured salmon. If you want to take this to the next level, then make it into smoked salmon! You can follow this recipe then cold-smoke it. Either way, it's delicious!

Serves 8-10 appetizer portions

2 lb (1kg) sushi-grade salmon fillet, skin on
½ cup kosher salt
¼ cup sugar
Zest of ½ a lemon
1 bunch of dill, chopped

א Place a big sheet of plastic wrap on the counter.

ב Rinse and dry the salmon. Place it on the plastic wrap. Sprinkle the salt, sugar, lemon zest and dill on the top, sides and bottom of the fish. Wrap it up.

ג Place it in a baking dish in the refrigerator (it's going to drip). Add a weight on top, such as a plate with a couple of cans on top of it (this makes the salting happen more evenly). Refrigerate for 48 hours.

ד Unwrap and rinse well. Cut thin slices with a long sharp knife.

ה Serve at brunch with bagels and cream cheese.

TIP
To find sushi-grade salmon, check a local fishmonger or Japanese market.

Pickled Fish

Serves 8-10 appetizer portions

FISH

2 trout fillets, previously frozen

½ lb (250 g) sushi-grade salmon fillet

BRINE

1½ cups water

1½ cups vinegar

¼ cup sugar

⅓ cup salt

IN THE JARS

1 head of garlic, peeled

3 teaspoons black peppercorns

3 bay leaves

1 red onion, sliced

3 tablespoons vegetable oil

א To make the brine, add the water and vinegar to a pot and bring to a boil. Remove from heat and dissolve the sugar and salt into the water.

ב Allow the brine to cool for 15 minutes.

ג Fill a few jars with some fish, 3 cloves of garlic, a teaspoon of black peppercorns, 1 bay leaf and the slices of ¼ red onion. Don't pack the jars tightly - the fish should have room to swim.

ד Add 1 tablespoon of vegetable oil to each jar then fill to the top with the brine. Close the jars and refrigerate for 48 hours. Serve with crackers and vodka shots.

TIP

Fresh herring is hard to find, but if you find it, use this same method.

Honey-Caramelized Salmon with Apple Arugula Salad

Apples & honey for Rosh Hashanah and all year 'round.

Serves 4

FOR THE SALAD

1 green apple, thinly sliced
5 radishes, thinly sliced
½ tablespoon lemon juice
5 oz (140 g) arugula
1 teaspoon honey
½ tablespoon olive oil
Salt and pepper

FOR THE SALMON

4 salmon fillets (skin on or off)
Salt and pepper
4 teaspoons honey
Pinch of chili flakes
2 tablespoons olive oil (for frying)

א Thinly slice the apple and radishes. Add to serving bowl along with the lemon juice, which prevents the apple from turning brown.

ב For the salmon, first dry the fillets with a paper towel. Sprinkle salt and pepper on both sides. Spread one teaspoon of honey on the side without skin. Sprinkle chili flakes.

ג Add 2 tablespoons of olive oil to a frying pan on medium heat. Once the oil is hot, add the salmon with the skin side up (so the honey side is directly on the pan). Cook for 30 seconds then check with a spatula if the honey-glazed side is caramelized. Once caramelized, flip and cook the skin side of the salmon for 3 minutes.

ד Mix the honey, oil, salt and pepper in a small bowl. Immediately before serving, add the arugula to a bowl, pour the dressing on top and toss gently.

SCHMIDT

Salmon Paella

Serves 6

2 tablespoons olive oil
3 cloves garlic, chopped
1 onion, finely chopped
1 red bell pepper, chopped
1 can diced tomatoes
1 teaspoon salt
1 tablespoon paprika
1 bay leaf
1 bunch green beans
3 teaspoons soup bouillon
Pinch of saffron
2½ cups water
1 cup paella rice, short-grain
1 lb (500 g) fresh salmon without skin

א Add olive oil to a very wide pan on medium heat. Fry the garlic, onion and pepper until softened, about 5 minutes.

ב Add the tomatoes, salt, paprika, bay leaf and green beans. Stir and cook until the sauce starts to thicken, about 5 minutes.

ג Add the bouillon, saffron, water and rice. Stir. Simmer for 5 minutes, stirring occasionally. Add more water if the sauce goes below the surface of the rice.

ד Place the salmon slices on top and press them into the sauce. Turn the heat to low and cover the pan with aluminum foil. Cook for 15 minutes or until rice is cooked through.

Moroccan Fish

Dana's family is from Tétouan, Morocco, which is heavily influenced by Spanish culture. That's why Dana's grandmother is called 'Abuela' and also why this fish recipe is a mash-up of garlicky Spanish cuisine and beautifully spiced Moroccan tagine.

Serves 4

4 tablespoons olive oil
1 red bell pepper, sliced
1 chili pepper, seeds removed and sliced
8 cloves garlic, peeled
1 can diced tomatoes (14.5 oz / 400 g)
1 can cooked chickpeas (14.5 oz / 400g), optional
1 cup chopped cilantro
1½ cups water
½ teaspoon salt
½ teaspoon cumin
2 tablespoons + 1 teaspoon sweet paprika
4 fish fillets, tilapia, salmon, grouper or your favorite fish
Juice of ½ lemon

א Add 1 tablespoon of olive oil to a large pot on medium heat. Add the peppers and cook for 10 minutes, stirring occasionally.

ב Add the garlic, diced tomatoes, chickpeas, half of the chopped cilantro, water, salt, cumin and 1 teaspoon of paprika. Mix, cover and cook for 10 minutes.

ג Meanwhile, add 3 tablespoon of olive oil to a large bowl. Add 2 tablespoons of paprika and a pinch of salt, then mix. Add each piece of fish to the mixture and flip to coat well.

ד Place the fish in the pot on top of the vegetables and pour the remaining oil on top. Squeeze half a lemon on top and throw in the other half of the cilantro. Simmer until the fish is cooked through.

ה Season with a pinch of salt and serve hot.

MEAT

בָּשָׂר
[Bahsar]

Chicken Soup

Your mother and the 12th century Jewish philosopher, Maimonides, have claimed that chicken soup has healing powers. You should listen to them. This recipe is soup-er flexible, so don't worry if you don't have the exact ingredients. Throw all your favorite herbs and veggies in the broth.

Serves 8

3-4 lb (1.5 kg) whole chicken, cut up (most stores sell chicken already cut up)
4 carrots
2 onions, halved
4 celery stalks
Small bunch of fresh parsley
3 cloves garlic
3 sprigs thyme
1 bay leaf
1 tablespoon black peppercorns
1 teaspoon salt
16 cups water

א Place all the ingredients in a large pot and cover completely with cold water, about 4 quarts (16 cups). Cook uncovered on medium heat for 90 minutes.

ב Let's make the matzo balls while the soup cooks (see next page).

ג Use tongs to remove the chicken, carrots and celery from the pot and set aside. Pick the meat off the bones and chop the vegetables.

ד Carefully strain the broth into another large pot or bowl.

ה Add the chicken and vegetables back into the soup and adjust salt to taste.

Matzo Balls

The super-fluffy kind.

Makes: 12 matzo balls

1 cup matzo meal
½ teaspoon salt
2 teaspoons baking powder
4 large eggs
4 tablespoons vegetable oil or schmaltz (rendered chicken fat)

א Mix the matzo meal, salt and baking powder in a large bowl.

ב In a separate bowl, gently mix the eggs and oil or schmaltz.

ג Add the egg mixture to the matzo meal mixture and gently mix until barely combined.

ד Place in the fridge until cooled, about 1 hour.

ה Bring a large pot of salted water to a boil.

ו Shape the mix into small balls.

ז Add them to the boiling water. Immediately turn the heat down to a simmer. Cover and cook for 35 minutes.

Meat-Stuffed Eggplant

Serves 2-4

2 eggplants
2 tablespoons olive oil
1 onion, finely chopped
½ lb (225 g) ground beef or lamb
¼ teaspoon cumin
Salt and pepper
1 red pepper, finely chopped
1 carrot, finely chopped

Tahini

4 tablespoons raw tahini
1 tablespoon lemon juice
Approx. 3 tablespoons water
¼ teaspoon salt, to taste

א Preheat oven to 400°F / 200°C.

ב Slice the eggplants in half lengthwise. Place cut-side up on a baking sheet and drizzle with olive oil and sprinkle with salt and pepper. Bake for 30 minutes. Some eggplants have bitter seeds, so when the they're finished cooking, taste the seeds and remove them with a spoon if necessary.

ג Meanwhile, heat olive oil in a pan on medium-high heat. Add half of the onion, the meat, cumin, salt and pepper. Break up the chunks of meat and cook until browned.

ד Remove the meat from the pan and set aside.

ה Add the other half of the onion, the red pepper and carrot. Cook the veggies for a few minutes on high heat until browned but not cooked all the way through, so they still have a nice crunch.

ו *FOR THE TAHINI:*
Add the raw tahini to a small bowl with the lemon juice. Gradually mix in water until it reaches a smooth consistency. Some brands of tahini are thicker than others, so adjust the water accordingly. Season with salt to taste.

ז Drizzle tahini on the eggplant. Scoop some meat on top, followed by the cooked veggies, and more tahini.

the best
Brisket

When it comes to brisket, you don't want to risk it.

Serves 6-8

4 lb (1.8 kg) brisket
2 tablespoons oil
2 onions, sliced
6 garlic cloves, whole and peeled
6 small carrots, 3 grated and 3 peeled
2 tablespoons tomato paste
2 teaspoons salt
½ teaspoon pepper
1 tablespoon paprika
Pinch cayenne pepper
1 cup red wine
2 cups chicken stock
¼ cup brown sugar
2 tablespoons white vinegar
6 celery stalks
1 bunch parsley
6 thyme sprigs
3 rosemary sprigs

א Preheat oven to 300°F / 150°C.

ב Heat the oil in a pot on medium heat. Once hot, add the onions and stir occasionally until golden, about 10v minutes. Add the garlic, grated carrots, tomato paste and spices (salt, pepper, paprika and cayenne pepper). Stir and cook for 5 more minutes.

ג Add the red wine, chicken stock, brown sugar and vinegar. Stir well to scrape up the caramelized flavor from the bottom of the pan. Remove from heat.

ד Place the meat in a baking dish and carefully pour the sauce (from the pot) on top.

ה Place the celery, 3 peeled carrots, parsley, thyme and rosemary into the dish around the meat. Cover with aluminum foil and bake for 4 hours (or 1 hour per pound of meat).

ו Allow the brisket to cool and remove it from the dish. Slice against the grain with a sharp knife. After the meat is sliced, place it back into the dish and reheat before serving.

TIP
Brisket is much easier to slice when cold. If you have time, refrigerate it before slicing.

Cholent

Jews from around the world have developed unique versions of slow-cooked Shabbat stews. For this Ashkenazi version, you better grab your fiddle and dancing shoes. This cholent is going to take you back to the 1800s. To recreate the flavors of our ancestors, we used simple ingredients that were available back in the 'shtetl' markets of Eastern Europe.

Serves 8

2 medium potatoes, peeled and chopped
1 onion, chopped
1½ lbs (700 g) stew meat, chuck or any fatty cut
4 garlic cloves, chopped
½ cup of barley
1 cup of mixed beans, kidney, pinto, navy
2 tablespoons sugar
2 teaspoons salt
½ teaspoon pepper
3 cups chicken broth

א In a slow cooker or an oven-proof pot, evenly layer the potatoes, onion, meat, garlic, barley and beans. Sprinkle the sugar, salt and pepper all over the top. Add the chicken stock. If the chicken stock doesn't cover the ingredients, add a little water.

ב Place in the oven on 200°F / 90°C for at least 12 hours (or in a slow cooker on low).

Orisa

This Shabbat treat from Morocco is packed with flavor. It's typically started on Friday afternoon and served for Shabbat lunch. The flavorful combination of the meat with the garlicky, paprika-soaked, sweet potatoes is unlike anything in Western cooking. Sephardic Shabbat dishes almost always include eggs, called 'huevos haminados', which turn brown after cooking at a low temperature for a long time.

Serves 8

⅓ cup olive oil
2 onions, chopped
1½ lbs (680 g) stew meat, chuck or any fatty cut
1½ cups barley or rice
1 tablespoon sweet paprika
2 tablespoons brown sugar
1½ teaspoons salt
8 garlic cloves, whole and peeled
2½ cups water
2 large sweet potatoes, cut into chunks
Eggs, one per person

א Heat olive oil in an oven-proof pot on medium heat. Once hot, add the onions. Stir occasionally until onions are soft, about 10 minutes.

ב Add the meat, barley (or rice), paprika, brown sugar, salt and garlic. Mix and cook for 2 minutes.

ג Pour in the water and place the sweet potatoes and eggs on top.

ד To serve the orisa that day, cover and cook on medium-low heat (closer to low) until the meat is soft, about 1½ hours. To serve for lunch the following day, place in the oven on 200°F / 90°C for 12 to 16 hours.

ה Peel the eggs before serving and place back on top of the orisa.

Mafrum

The Libyan Jewish community dates back more than 2,000 years. In 2003, the last Jew of Libya left the country. This incredibly flavorful Jewish-Libyan dish throws us back in time.

Serves 6-8

5 potatoes
1 cup flour
2 large eggs
2 tablespoons vegetable oil, for frying

MEAT FILLING
1 lb (450 g) ground beef
½ cup parsley, chopped
2 large eggs
½ large onion, chopped
⅓ cup breadcrumbs
¼ teaspoon cinnamon
¼ teaspoon cumin
2 teaspoons paprika
1 teaspoon salt
½ teaspoon black pepper

SAUCE
1 tablespoon vegetable oil
1 small onion, chopped
2 cloves garlic, chopped
2 tablespoons paprika
⅓ cup tomato paste
2 cups water
3 tomatoes, chopped
1 teaspoon salt
½ teaspoon black pepper

א Peel the potatoes and cut into ½ inch (1¼ cm) thick slices. Cut into each slice of potato to make a V shape (see picture). Place the sliced potatoes in a bowl of water to keep fresh.

ב Mix all the meat filling ingredients in a bowl. Take golf-ball sized balls of the meat and stuff them into the potato slices.

ג Roll the stuffed potatoes in flour, then in the beaten eggs.

ד Add 2 tablespoons of oil to a pan and fry the potatoes on medium heat until golden. Flip to fry on all sides.

ה For the sauce, add oil to a pot on medium heat. Use a pot that has a lid. Cook the onion, garlic and paprika for 2 minutes. Stir frequently so that the paprika doesn't burn. Add the water, tomato paste, chopped tomatoes, salt and pepper. Mix.

ו Add the fried potatoes, cover and cook on low heat for 45 mins. Serve with couscous.

Hassleback Salami

There's a selection of Jewish-American recipes that don't necessarily have a connection with traditional Jewish life. This epic party appetizer fits right into that category.

Serves 6-8 appetizer portions

14-16 oz (425 g) salami
½ cup apricot jam
½ tablespoon hot sauce
1 tablespoon maple syrup
1 tablespoon brown sugar

א Preheat the oven to 400°F / 200°C. Place two chopsticks on both sides of the salami (with plastic removed).

ב Cut thin slices, about ⅛ inch thick. The chopsticks prevent the knife from cutting completely through the salami.

ג Mix the apricot jam, hot sauce, maple syrup and brown sugar in a bowl.

ד Pour over the salami. Make sure it gets in between the slices.

ה Bake for 45 minutes or until crisped to your liking. Every 15 minutes, remove it from the oven and scoop some of the sauce onto the salami. That keeps it nice and juicy.

ו To serve, place on a platter with a knife so people can help themselves. Set a dish of mustard on the side.

Steak-Stuffed Pita Fajita

Serves 6

6 pitas
1 lb (½ kg) skirt steak
2 tablespoons vegetable oil
Salt and pepper
1 small onion, chopped
1 small red bell pepper, sliced
1 small yellow bell pepper, sliced
1 small green bell pepper, sliced

SALAD
1 cup chopped parsley
2 cloves garlic, chopped
2 tomatoes, chopped
1 tablespoon olive oil
Juice of ½ lemon
Salt and pepper

DON'T FORGET
Tahini
Israeli pickles
Harissa/schug (spicy chili paste)

א Heat 1 tablespoon of oil in a pan on high heat.

ב Rub steak with salt and pepper on both sides.

ג When the pan is very hot, carefully place the steak. Cook for 3 minutes. Flip and cook for 3 minutes on the other side. Set the steak aside to rest for 5 minutes. Slice it against the grain into strips (this makes the steak more tender).

ד Add more oil to the pan if there isn't any left. Add onions and peppers. Cook until veggies are caramelized but still crunchy, about 7 minutes.

ה For the salad, mix the parsley, garlic, tomatoes, olive oil, lemon juice, salt and pepper.

ו Slice each pita at the top and open it up with your fingers. Stuff it with tons of tahini, salad, steak, pickles, schug (spicy chili paste).

*Making Matzah for Passover

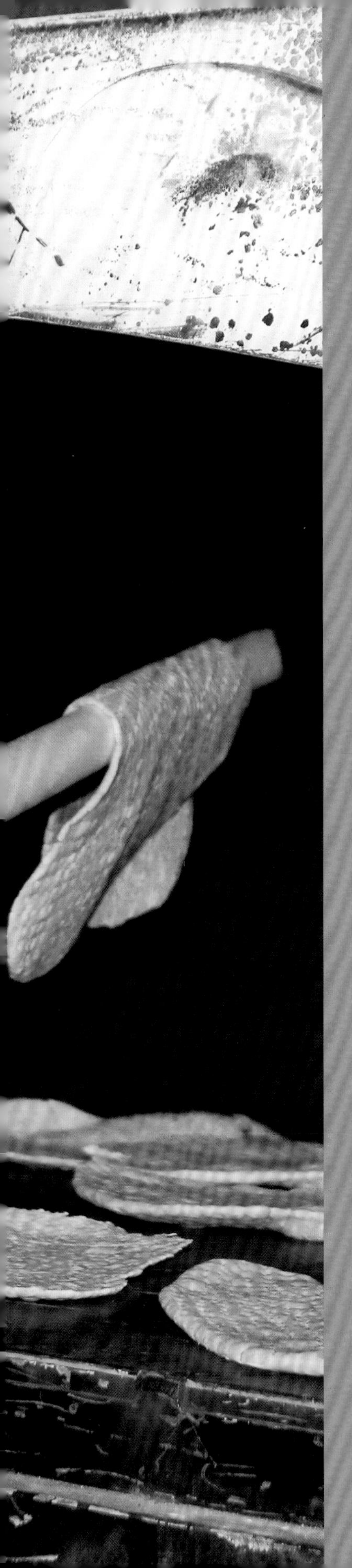

HOLIDAYS

חַגִים
[Hag-eem] - with a hard h

Apple Challah Bread Pudding

Rosh Hashana

Serves 6-8

3 large eggs
2 cups milk
1½ teaspoons cinnamon
1 teaspoons vanilla
½ large challah
1 tablespoon butter
1½ tablespoons honey
2 Granny Smith apples, cored and chopped
½ cup pomegranate seeds (optional)

א Preheat oven to 350°F / 175°C. Cut challah into cubes.

ב In a large bowl, whisk the eggs, milk, cinnamon and vanilla. Add challah and soak for 30 minutes. This gives the bread its delicious custard-like texture.

ג In a pan, melt the butter on medium-high heat. Add the honey and apples. Mix. Cook for about 5 minutes until the apples start to caramelize. Remove from heat, add the pomegranate seeds (optional) and mix.

ד Add the challah mixture to a greased 8 by 8 inch baking dish and spread evenly. Pour the apple mixture on top and spread.

ה Bake for 40 minutes, or until browned on top. Serve with a drizzle of honey or maple syrup and garnish with fresh pomegranate seeds.

Rosh Hashana

Makes: 2 cakes

3 cups flour
1 teaspoon baking powder
1 teaspoon baking soda
1 teaspoon kosher salt
¼ cup white sugar
½ cup brown sugar
1 cup vegetable oil
¾ cup honey
2 large eggs
1 teaspoon vanilla
1 cup orange juice
1 Granny Smith apple, peeled and sliced

א Preheat oven to 325°F / 160°C.

ב Mix the flour, baking powder, baking soda and salt in a large bowl.

ג Add everything else except the apples and mix again.

ד Grease 2 loaf pans and place apple slices on the bottom. In each pan, pour some of the batter, then another layer of apples and finally the remaining batter. Place any remaining apple slices on top. The batter should fill halfway to the top of the pan. This cake rises a lot!

ה Bake for 50 minutes or until you can insert a knife into the center of the cake and remove it clean. Let the cakes to cool for 10 minutes, then flip them out of the pans.

Apple Honey Cake

Crispy Potato Latkes

Hanukkah

Makes: 24 latkes

3 large potatoes, peeled
1 small onion, peeled
2 large eggs
3 tablespoons flour
½ teaspoon salt
½ teaspoon black pepper
Oil, for frying

TOPPING
Applesauce
Sour cream

א Grate the potatoes and the onion using a hand grater or with the grater attachment on a food processor.

ב Place the grated potatoes and onion in a cloth and squeeze out all the liquid. This is the trick for making the latkes extra crispy, so make sure to squeeze really well.

ג Add the potatoes and the onion to a large bowl along with the eggs, flour, salt and pepper. Mix well.

ד Pour oil into a wide pan so it coats the entire surface. Place on medium heat. Once the oil is hot, scoop a spoonful of the mixture and place in the pan. Press down with the back of the spoon or a spatula to make it flat. Fry for about 2 minutes on each side until crispy.

ה Place the cooked latkes on paper towels to soak up the excess oil. Keep in a warm oven until serving. Serve with applesauce and sour cream.

Cheesy Sweet Potato Latkes

Hanukkah

Makes: 12 latkes

2 large sweet potatoes, peeled
3 green onions, chopped
2 large eggs
3 tablespoons flour
½ teaspoon salt
½ teaspoon black pepper
4 oz (110 g) cheese of your choice, shredded (we use mozzarella)
Oil, for frying

TOPPING
Sour cream
Green onion, chopped

א Grate the sweet potatoes using a hand grater or with the grater attachment on a food processor.

ב Place the grated sweet potatoes in a kitchen towel. Squeeze out as much liquid as you can. Sweet potatoes are tough, so use your muscles! The more you squeeze, the crispier the latkes.

ג Mix the potatoes in a large bowl with the green onions, eggs, flour, salt and pepper.

ד Pour oil into a wide pan so it coats the entire surface. Place on medium-low heat. Place a spoonful of the mixture in the pan. Press it down with the back of the spoon or a spatula to make it flat. Place a pinch of shredded cheese on top. Place another spoonful of the mixture on top and press it down again. Cook on each side for 5 to 7 minutes. If the latkes are burning before 5 minutes, turn the heat down a little.

ה Place the cooked sweet potato latkes on paper towels to drain the excess oil. Keep in a warm oven until serving. Serve with sour cream and chopped green onion.

Hanukkah

Makes: 12 doughnuts

1 large egg
1½ tablespoons vegetable oil + more for deep-frying
2¼ teaspoons active dry yeast (1 packet)
½ teaspoon vanilla extract
3 tablespoons sugar
Pinch of salt
¾ cup warm water
3 cups all-purpose flour
1-2 cups of strawberry jelly
Powdered sugar

א In a gallon-sized ziplock bag, add the egg, oil, yeast, vanilla, sugar, salt and warm water. Zip and shake to mix. Add the flour. Zip the bag and squeeze to mix the ingredients and knead the dough for about 5 minutes, until all the ingredients are mixed well.

ב Place the bag in a bowl of very warm water to rise for 30 minutes.

ג Remove the dough from the bag and shape it into a cylinder. Cut the dough into 12 even pieces and roll each one on the table into a smooth ball. Place each ball of dough on a floured surface. Leave plenty of space between them since they double in size. Cover with a towel and allow the doughnuts to rise for 45 minutes.

ד Fill a large pot with 2 inches (5 cm) of oil and bring to 350°F / 175°C. If you don't have a thermometer, then set the flame to medium heat and add the first doughnut. It should bubble and float to the top. Using a spatula, gently transfer some of the doughnuts into the oil. Cook for about 2 minutes on each side until golden. If the oil is too hot, they will turn brown in less than two minutes and the inside will remain uncooked, so adjust the heat accordingly.

ה Remove and set on paper towels. With a squeeze tube or a piping bag, squeeze jelly into the top of the doughnuts. Dust with powdered sugar.

Sufganiyot in a Bag

These crispy sugar-coated pastries are eated on Purim and after fasting on Yom Kippur. Thanks to her Abuela (grandmother), we were able to learn the traditional technique of twisting the dough in the oil. Although Dana grew up calling these 'fijuelas', Tunisians call them 'deblas' and others call them 'fazuelos'. Apparently, desserts names is a touchy subject in North African countries.

Makes: 12 pastries

2 large eggs
1 teaspoon baking powder
½ teaspoon salt
1 tablespoon sugar
2 tablespoons vegetable oil
1 tablespoon water
1½ cups flour

SYRUP

1 cup sugar
1 cup water
1 tablespoon honey
1 tablespoon lemon juice

א Mix the eggs, baking powder, salt, sugar, oil and water in a large bowl. Gradually add the flour and mix until the dough is smooth (you can use your hands). Add more flour, 1 tablespoon at a time if the dough feels too wet to work with.

ב Sprinkle flour on the counter. Using a rolling pin or a pasta maker, roll the dough out as this as you possibly can. Cut into 1 inch wide strips.

ג Fill a frying pan with ½ inch of oil. Place on high heat for 2 minutes, then decrease the heat to low.

ד Now for the tricky part. Insert one strip of dough in between the prongs of a fork (see photos).

ה While holding the long end, dip the fork into the oil and let it fry for several seconds until crispy. Twist the fork, rolling the dough so that a new part is exposed to the oil. Keep twisting until golden all the way around. Remove and let the fijuelas drain on paper towels.

ו For the syrup, heat the sugar, water, honey and lemon juice in a saucepan on medium heat. Stir until dissolved then simmer for 5 minutes. Individually dip each cooked fijuela into the syrup pan and tilt the pan so the syrup covers the fijuela completely.

Fijuelas

Abigail's Peanut Butter & Chocolate Hamantaschen

"These are my favorite because they have my two favorite things in them. chocolate AND peanut butter. Oh, and the rainbow sprinkles."
- Abigail, 9 years old, said in her adorable British accent.

Purim

Makes: 20

8 tablespoons butter, softened
2 tablespoon sugar
4 tablespoons Nutella
2 cups flour
Approx. 6 teaspoons water
Peanut butter, sweetened (or Nutella)
Rainbow sprinkles

א Preheat the oven to 350°F / 175°C. Add the butter and sugar to a bowl. Mix until fluffy.

ב Add the Nutella. Mix.

ג Add the flour. Mix until it becomes a powder.

ד Mix in one teaspoon of water at a time until a crumbly dough forms.

ה Squeeze into a ball with your hands.

ו Place the dough on a big sheet of plastic wrap. Place another piece of plastic over the dough. Roll the dough to ¼ inch thickness (½ cm) with a rolling pin. Remove the top sheet of plastic and cut 3 inch (7½ cm) circles with a cup.

ז Remove excess dough and transfer circles to a lined baking sheet. Repeat with the extra dough.

ח Place a teaspoon (no more than that) of peanut butter or Nutella in the center, fold the 3 sides and pinch the corners tightly. Top with rainbow sprinkles and bake for 15 minutes.

TIP
If you put too much filling, they might open up while baking.

Chocolate Matzah Crunch

Passover

Serves 8

4-5 sheets of matzah
1 cup butter
1 cup brown sugar
1 cup chocolate chips

TOPPING IDEAS
Sea salt
Sliced almonds
Crushed pretzels

א Preheat oven to 350°F / 175°C.

ב Cover a tray with baking paper. Fill the tray with one layer of matzah, breaking them to fit the entire tray.

ג Melt butter and brown sugar in a pot over medium heat. Stir constantly and bring to a boil. Boil for 3 minutes, stirring often.

ד Pour the toffee over the matzah and spread evenly with a spatula.

ה Bake for 12 minutes. Keep an eye on it and don't let it burn.

ו While the matzah is still hot, sprinkle the chocolate chips on top and let it sit for 5 minutes. Spread the chocolate with a spatula. Sprinkle your favorite crazy toppings.

ז Once it comes to room temperature, place it in the freezer for 30 minutes.

ח Cut into smaller pieces and place them in an airtight container. Store in the refrigerator or freezer and serve cold (the chocolate is less messy when cold).

Pizza-Brei

This twist on the classic 'Matzo brei' is a fun addition to the old-school Passover recipe list.

Serves 2

2 sheets matzah
4 large eggs
Salt & pepper
1 tablespoon butter
4 tablespoons pizza sauce
½ cup mozzarella, shredded

א Soak the matzah in water for 30 seconds. Remove and shake off the excess water.

ב Scramble the eggs in a bowl with the salt and pepper.

ג Melt the butter in a frying pan on medium heat. Break the matzah into chunky pieces and add it to the pan. Pour in the egg mixture. Flatten the eggs and matzah with a spatula. Cover and cook on low heat for 5 minutes.

ד Remove the cover then flip the matzah pancake onto a plate. Add it back into the pan so the cooked side is facing up. Spread the tomato sauce on top. Sprinkle the mozzarella along with your other favorite toppings. Cover and cook on low heat for a few more minutes, until the cheese is melted.

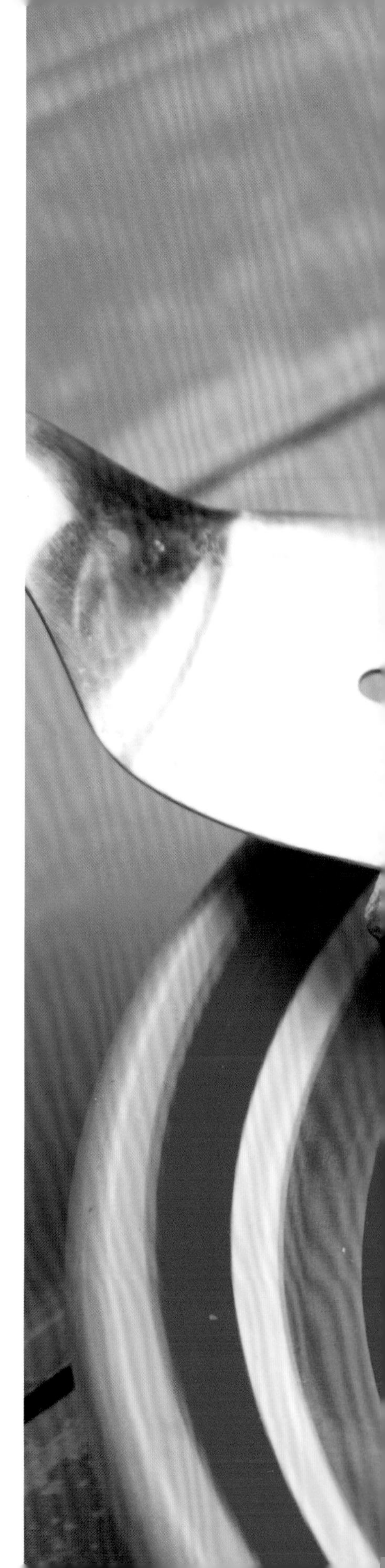

Matzah Lasagna

Passover

Serves 6

1 tablespoon olive oil
3 sheets of matzah
½ onion, chopped
½ bell pepper, chopped
3 cloves of garlic, chopped
1 zucchini (1½ cups), sliced
28 oz (800 g) tomato sauce
Small bunch fresh basil
Salt and pepper
12 oz (300 g) ricotta cheese, shredded
12 oz (300 g) mozzarella cheese, shredded
4 oz (110 g) Parmesan cheese, shredded

א Preheat oven to 350°F / 175°C. Heat olive oil on medium heat in a large pan. Cook the onion and bell pepper until soft, about 10 minutes.

ב Add the garlic and zucchini. Cook for 3 minutes, stirring occasionally. Pour in a jar of your favorite tomato sauce and toss in some fresh basil. Remove from heat and add salt and pepper to taste.

ג Spread a thin layer of the tomato sauce on the bottom of an 8 by 8 inch baking dish.

ד Soak 3 sheets of matzah for 30 seconds in warm water. Shake off the excess water. Place one sheet of matzah on top of the sauce. If you're using a wider dish, you might need more matzah to fill the shape. Spread ⅓ of the ricotta on the matzah, followed by ⅓ of the mozzarella and ⅓ of the Parmesan. Spread another layer of sauce then repeat.

ה Bake for 35 to 45 minutes until crisped to your preference.

On the night when Passover ends, Moroccan Jewish families celebrate with a special 'Mimouna party'. Every Mimouna party needs two things: people shouting 'kulululululu!' and freshly cooked moufleta. Traditionally, Mimouna was a time when Muslim neighbors brought gifts of fresh flowers, milk and fruit to their Jewish friends in Morocco. Tables were decorated with gold coins and fresh fish to symbolize prosperity and fertility. It was a time for seeing friends and celebrating. In Israel today, Moroccans still celebrate Mimouna, and it's a party that everyone wants to be invited to!

Passover

Makes: about 20

3½ cups flour
1 teaspoon kosher salt
1 teaspoon sugar
1½ cups warm water
½ cup vegetable oil

TOPPING
Butter
Honey

א Mix the flour, salt and sugar in a large bowl. Add the water and mix until a dough forms. Knead until smooth, about 5 minutes.

ב Using your thumb and forefinger, pinch a small ball of dough and place on a large tray covered with oil. Flip the dough balls in the oil so they don't dry out. Repeat with all the dough. Cover the dough and let it rest for 20 minutes.

ג Starting with the balls that were rolled first, take one and place it on a smooth surface. With well-oiled hands, flatten and stretch the dough into a very thin circle. If it tears easily, let it rest for 10 more minutes and try again.

ד Place the first moufleta in a large frying pan on medium-low heat. Cook for about 3 minutes while you flatten the second moufleta. When the first one is golden brown, flip it over. This is the only moufleta that is cooked on both sides! Moufletas are cooked in a stack which keeps them hot until serving. Place the second moufleta on top and flip the stack. While the second moufleta is cooking, flatten the third moufleta. Place the third moufleta on top then flip. Repeat until the stack is difficult to flip, then start a new stack.

ה Serve hot with butter and honey for spreading.

Moufleta for the Mimouna Party

Oreo Cheesecake

Israel is known as the land of 'milk and honey', so it's no surprise that there is a holiday during which we eat tons of cheesy food.

Shavuot

Serves 8

CRUST

40 Oreos, crushed, or 3½ cups of graham cracker crumbs

8 tablespoons butter, melted

CHEESECAKE

24 oz (680 g) cream cheese

1½ cups sugar

4 large eggs, separated

1 tablespoon lemon juice

1 teaspoon vanilla

א Preheat the oven to 325°F / 160°C.

ב For the crust, either grind the Oreos (or graham crackers) in a food processor or crush them in a plastic bag with a rolling pin.

ג Mix the crumbs with the melted butter. Add the mixture to a 9 inch springform pan. Using a measuring cup, press the crumbs firmly against the bottom and sides of the pan to form a crust.

ד In a bowl, use a hand mixer to combine the cream cheese, sugar, egg yolks, lemon juice and vanilla.

ה In another bowl, use a hand mixer to mix the egg whites until they become stiff and fluffy (that's called 'stiff peaks').

ו Scoop the egg whites into the cream cheese mixture and gently mix with a spatula. Pour into the pan and use the spatula to flatten the top.

ז Bake for 35 minutes. Turn off the oven and let it sit for 1 hour. Don't open the oven door.

ח Freeze the cheesecake for at least 3 hours. Remove it from the pan while frozen.

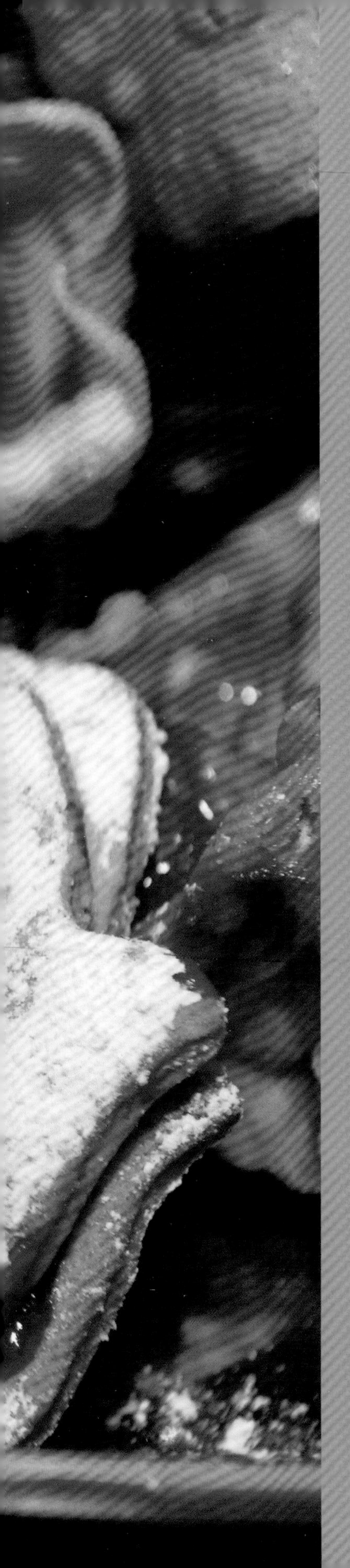

DESSERT

קִנּוּחַ
[Kinuah] - with a hard h

TAHINI COOKIES

DAIRY-FREE CHOCOLATE
CHIP COOKIES

CHOCOLATE RUGELACH IN A BAG

MALABI (ROSEWATER PUDDING)

COCONUT MERINGUE MONSTER
COOKIES

CHOCOLATE BABKA IN A BAG

BAKLAVA

These cookies are crisp on the outside and chewy on the inside. Dunk them into a cup of strong black coffee, change your name to Yuval, and wham! Suddenly you're the most Israeli person you know.

Makes: 12

⅔ cup raw tahini
1 teaspoon vanilla
1 large egg
⅔ cup sugar
1 teaspoon baking powder
Pinch of salt
½ cup flour

א Preheat the oven to 350°F / 175°C.

ב Mix all ingredients except the flour in a bowl.

ג Add the flour and mix until it feels crumbly.

ד Using your hands, take a small handful of the crumbly dough and squeeze it into a ball. Place it on a parchment lined baking sheet. Repeat with the remaining dough.

ה Use your thumb to make an indent in the center of each cookie and place an almond there. Or, use a fork to slightly flatten each ball and make pretty lines.

ו Bake for 12 minutes. Give these cookies plenty of time to cool before eating. They stay fresh for several days. Delicious with coffee and tea!

Tahini Cookies

Dairy-Free Chocolate Chip Cookies

These chewy cookies are dairy-free, so they are Kosher to eat after meat meals. We make them almost every Shabbat!

Makes: 16 cookies

1½ cups flour
½ teaspoon baking soda
½ cup white sugar
½ cup brown sugar
½ teaspoon salt
1 large egg
½ cup oil
1 teaspoon vanilla
½ cup non-dairy chocolate chips

א Preheat the oven to 350°F / 175°C.

ב In a large bowl, mix the flour, baking soda, white sugar, brown sugar and salt with a fork.

ג In a separate small bowl, mix the egg, oil and vanilla with a fork. Add the egg mixture to the dry ingredients and mix well. Add the chocolate chips and mix again.

ד With your hands, squeeze the dough into balls then flatten into disks. Place them on a non-stick baking sheet. Bake for 12 minutes.

ה Allow to cool completely before digging in so they don't crumble!

Chocolate Rugelach in a Bag

Most American-style rugelach are crisp. This Israeli-style version is reminiscent of those from the markets in Jerusalem: soft, chocolatey and gooey.

Makes: 30 rugelach

DOUGH

1 large egg + 1 more for basting
¼ cup melted butter (or vegetable oil)
⅓ cup warm milk (or water)
½ teaspoon vanilla
2¼ teaspoons active dry yeast (1 packet)
2½ tablespoons sugar
½ teaspoon salt
1¾ cups flour

FILLING

¼ cup chocolate chips
¼ cup butter, (or vegetable oil)
¼ cup sugar
1 tablespoon cocoa powder

SYRUP

¼ cup water
⅓ cup sugar

א Add all the dough ingredients into a gallon-sized bag. Squeeze and knead for 5 minutes until the dough is evenly mixed.

ב Place the bag in a bowl of warm water to rise for 45 minutes.

ג Preheat the oven to 350°F / 175°C. For the filling, melt the chocolate chips and the butter in the microwave for 30 seconds. Then add the sugar and cocoa powder. Mix.

ד Dust a work surface with flour. Separate the dough into 3 even balls. Roll out the first ball into a super thin circle. If the dough is sticking to the table, dust the dough with flour and flip it over. Place a plate on top of the dough. Cut around it and remove the excess dough.

ה Spread ¼ of the filling on the dough. Cut it into 8 slices like a pizza. Separate one slice from the 'pizza' and roll it up. Place it on a non-stick baking tray. Repeat with the remaining dough and slices.

ו Brush with a beaten egg and bake until golden, about 15 to 20 minutes.

ז Meanwhile, make the glaze by combining the water and sugar in a saucepan on medium heat. Stir until the sugar melts, then remove from heat. When the rugelach are done baking, brush the glaze onto the rugelach, which will soak up the liquid as they cool.

Malabi
~Rosewater Pudding~

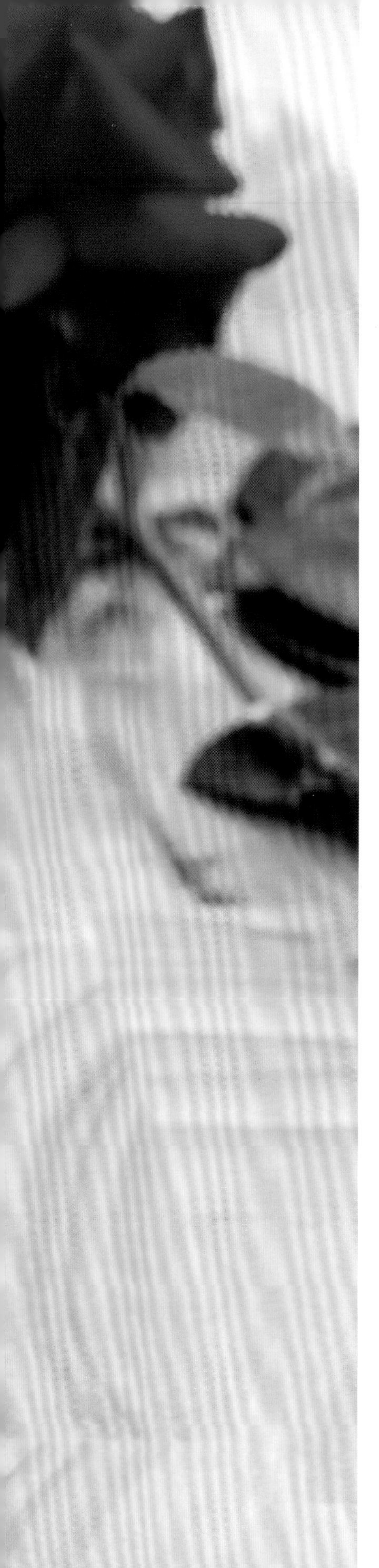

Legend has it that a 17th century Persian chef served this dessert to a Turkish general named Al-Muhallab. He liked it so much that he named it after himself. In Israel today, malabi is served at both upscale restaurants and small corner shops. For a winter version called 'sahlab', serve hot with a sprinkle of cinnamon.

Serves 3-4

PUDDING

1½ cups milk
⅓ cup sugar
3 tablespoons cornstarch
½ cup cold water
½ tablespoon rosewater
½ cup heavy cream

SYRUP

¼ cup sugar
¼ cup pomegranate juice
½ teaspoon rosewater

TOPPINGS

Shredded coconut
Chopped pistachios

א Add the milk and sugar to a pot on medium heat. Stir until the sugar dissolves. In a small bowl, mix the cornstarch and water.

ב When the milk comes to a simmer, turn the heat to medium-low and add the cornstarch mixture. Cook for 5 minutes, stirring often.

ג Remove from heat. Add the rosewater and heavy cream. Use a whisk to mix and remove any clumps. For a hot pudding (sahlab), serve immediately with a sprinkle of cinnamon.

ד For a cold pudding (malabi), scoop the mixture into small cups and refrigerate for several hours until solid.

ה For the syrup, mix all the ingredients over medium heat. Once it comes to a boil, allow it to bubble for 3 minutes, stirring occasionally. Cool completely.

ו Before serving, pour some of the syrup on top of the malabi. Sprinkle with the coconut and pistachios.

Coconut Meringue Monster Cookies

Makes: 8 big meringues

1¾ cup sugar
5 large egg whites
½ teaspoon cocoa powder
Pinch of salt
¾ cup unsweetened shredded coconut
3 oz (80 g) dark chocolate, grated

TOPPINGS

2 oz (50 g) dark chocolate, grated
½ teaspoon cocoa powder

א Preheat oven to 400°F / 200°C.

ב Pour sugar onto a parchment lined baking sheet. Bake the sugar for 7 minutes.

ג Meanwhile, using an electric mixer, beat the egg whites on medium speed until foamy. Once the sugar is hot, reduce the oven temperature to 225°F / 110° C. Remove the sugar from the oven. Then carefully grasp the ends of the parchment paper and pinch one side to make a 'scooper'. Pour half of the sugar into the whipped egg whites. Continue to whip the eggs for 30 seconds then add the second half of the sugar. Continue to mix on medium-high speed until the merengue can hold a peak.

ד Sift the cocoa powder across the top of the meringue. Sprinkle the coconut and salt across the top too. Gently fold the meringue with a spatula two or three times. You don't want to mix it, just fold it into layers.

ה Prepare a parchment-lined baking sheet. With a spatula, scoop 8 meringues. Use a spoon to gently push the meringue off the spatula onto the tray. Use the spoon to make a pretty-looking peak on each meringue.

ו For the toppings, sift some cocoa powder and sprinkle grated chocolate.

ז Bake for 1½ hours. The inside should be gooey and delicious.

Chocolate Babka in a Bag

Makes: 1

DOUGH

2¼ teaspoons active dry yeast (1 packet)
⅓ cup warm water
1 large egg
2 tablespoons sugar
½ teaspoon orange zest
⅛ teaspoon kosher salt
2 tablespoons butter or 1½ tablespoons vegetable oil
⅛ teaspoon vanilla
1¾ cups flour

FILLING

13 oz (370g) Nutella
⅓ cup semi-sweet chocolate chips
Chopped nuts (optional)

Glaze

¼ cup water

א Add all the dough ingredients into a gallon-sized ziplock bag. Squeeze and knead for 5 minutes until the dough is evenly mixed.

ב Place the bag in a bowl of warm water to rise for 45 minutes.

ג Remove the dough from the bag onto a floured surface. Roll it out into a 12 by 12 inch square. Spread the Nutella, leaving a little space around the edges. Sprinkle the chocolate chips.

ד Roll it up from the bottom. Slice the roll in half, longways, so the chocolate is exposed.

ה Turn the halves so the chocolate sides are facing up. Bring one half over the other so they are crossed in the middle. Continue to cross the dough until the twist is complete. Place the babka in a greased 8 inch loaf pan, tucking the ends so it fits.

ו Place the babka in a warm spot in the kitchen and allow to rise until it fills the pan and becomes poofy! This takes at least 1 hour. Preheat the oven to 350°F / 175°C.

ז Bake for 40 minutes.

ח To make the glaze, combine the sugar and water in a saucepan over medium heat. Bring to a simmer and dissolve the sugar. When the babka is ready, brush it with the glaze. Once cool enough to handle, remove it from the pan.

Baklava

Makes: 30 pieces

1 package filo dough (usually 1 lb / 500 g)
¾ cup vegetable oil or 1½ sticks melted butter
3.5 oz (100 g) chopped pistachios for garnish

FILLING

1 lb (450 g) finely chopped almonds or mixed nuts
¼ cup white sugar
1 teaspoon cinnamon
¼ teaspoon cardamom

SYRUP

1 cup sugar
¾ cup water
½ cup honey
2 tablespoons lemon juice

א Defrost the filo dough according to the instructions on the package. Trust them. They know what's up when it comes to defrosting dough.

ב Preheat the oven to 350°F / 175°C. For the filling, mix the nuts, sugar, cinnamon and cardamom in a bowl. Cover the stack of filo dough with plastic wrap and a towel while you aren't working with it. This prevents it from drying out (which happens quickly).

ג Brush the inside of a wide baking dish with oil (or butter). Place one sheet of filo dough into the dish. Then brush more oil on top of that sheet. Repeat with 7 more sheets, bushing between each one. Scoop half of the nuts into the dish and spread evenly.

ד Place 8 more sheets of dough, brushing each one with oil or butter between the layers. Add the second half of the nuts and spread evenly. On top of that goes 8 more sheets of filo dough, brushing each one, and finally, brush the top layer.

ה Make 4 lengthwise cuts across the pan. Make diagonal cuts across the pan the other way. Sprinkle the top with some cold water, which prevents the filo from curling. Bake for 30 to 40 minutes until the top is golden.

ו Make the syrup right away. Add the sugar, water, honey and lemon juice to a small pot on medium heat. Stir until the sugar dissolves then simmer for 5 minutes. Remove from heat and allow it to cool.

ז Once the baklava is removed from the oven, pour the cooled syrup evenly over the top. Let it rest for 4 hours to soak up the liquid.

DOWN TOWN

LOW PRICES
35%
הנחה
מתנה
1+1

Acknowledgements

To Safta, Grandma and Grandpa, Abuela y Abuelo, Mimi and Papa. The ones we look up to the most. We love you.

To Cindy, our expert mom-chef, who instilled in us a love of food. You're always there for us and we'd be lost without you.

To Raquel, the coolest person we know, who helped with Jewlish so much. When we had a small question, you always went over the top to help. We can always count on you.

To Michal, Levy, David and Abigail, who are always laughing and loving. Your recipe testing (tasting) and confidence in us means the world.

To Michael, Ellie, Sam and Jojo, who encouraged us every step of the way. Your ideas helped us solve problems big and small.

To the Goldberg family, the 100-person support team. You believed in us from the beginning. This wouldn't have been possible without you. Wish we could mention each and every name.

To Bendaliavitz, our amazing Israeli family. We can always count on you to make us laugh and tell us what you really think. Thank you for loving Jewlish from the start.

To all our incredible family and friends from Israel, Los Angeles, Cleveland, London and beyond. Thank you for all the love and support.

Safta Dina: The first police woman of Israel

Dana's great-grandmother

By: Ronit Dassa, Dana's aunt

My grandmother, Dina Dassa-Lyons, was born in Poland in 1910, a time of great antisemitism. At 16, she joined the Zionist youth movement and went to live in Israel, where she met and married my grandad. He worked as a policeman in the British-established Palestine police force, which was part of the British colonial police service.

In 1940, my grandad died from a gunshot, leaving my grandma with five kids, one of whom was a newborn baby. My grandmother was an amazing, strong and resourceful woman, and when she was offered my grandad's job in the police force, she promptly accepted. She joined the Palestine police force, becoming its first female policewoman. My brother now works as a policeman in the Israeli police force, where he gets to see this picture every day, as it hangs proudly in the Jerusalem police headquarters.

My grandmother lived a long life – she died at 89 – having got remarried, to a British soldier, eventually moving with him to London. I love her sweet smile in this photo as she sits calmly, the only woman in an assembly of men.

מזל
LUCK
אהבה
LOVE
חיים
LIFE

About the Authors

Having spent most of her life moving between London and Israel, Dana has both a cheeky British side and an outgoing Israeli side. After receiving her degree in finance (with honors) from IDC Herzliya, Dana travelled the world and soaked up its flavor. Her favorite dishes are: fried fish in Spain, pasta in Italy, curry in India, tacos in Mexico and of course, shakshuka in Israel. Dana's vision for Jewlish is what makes it so diverse.

FUN FACT: The garment in the photo above is embroidered entirely with gold-thread. It belonged to Dana's great-grandmother and every bride in her family wears it at their Henna party (a Moroccan pre-wedding celebration).

Jacob moved from Cleveland, Ohio to Israel where he found the two loves of his life, Israeli cuisine and Dana. His love for food began during the years he worked at his mom's catering company, schlepping stacks of plates, smoking salmon and baking bread. In Israel, Jacob founded a digital media company that grew to 5 million monthly users and $5m yearly revenue. He wanted to find a way to blend food into his business, and so, Jewlish was born.

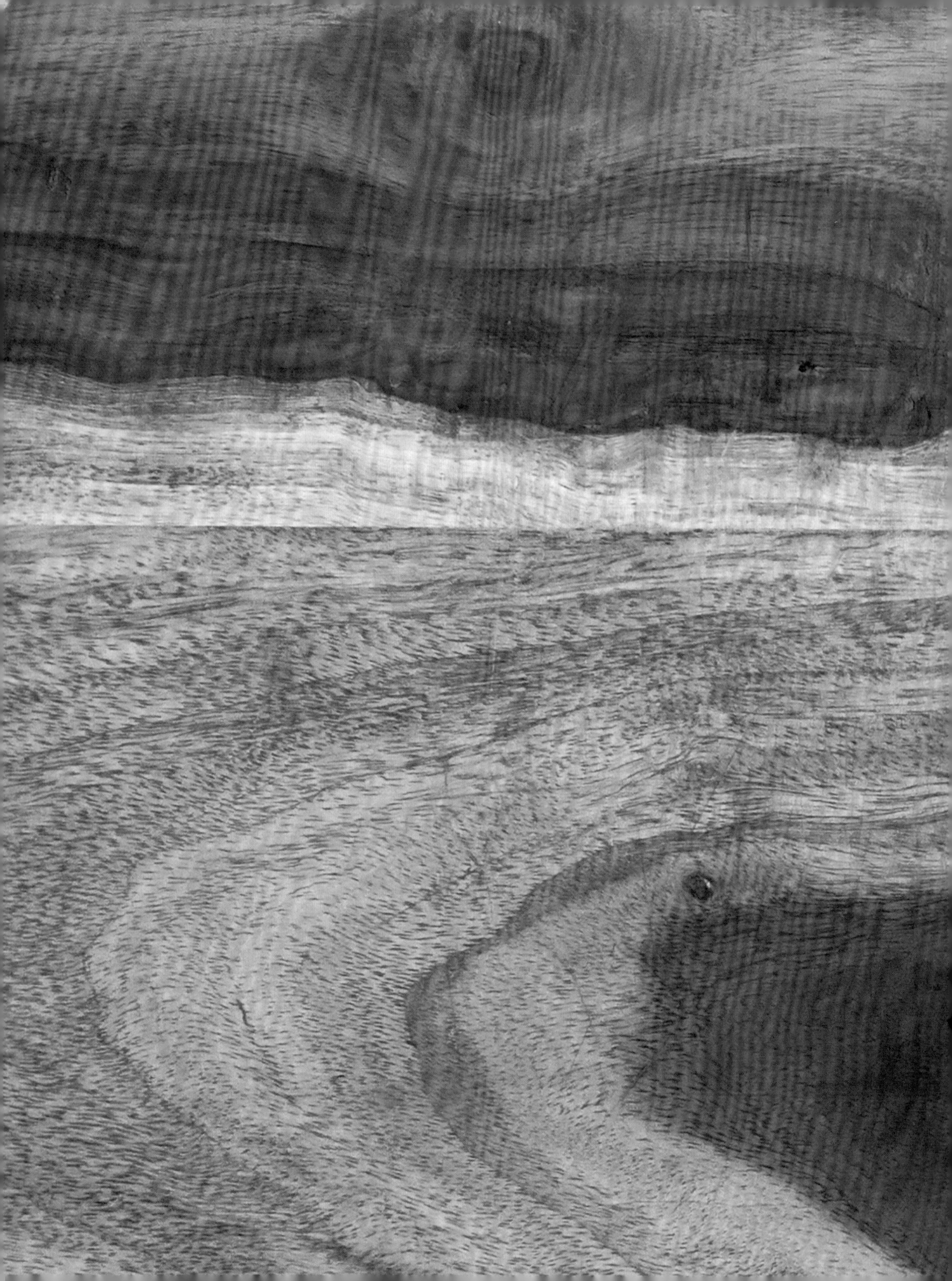

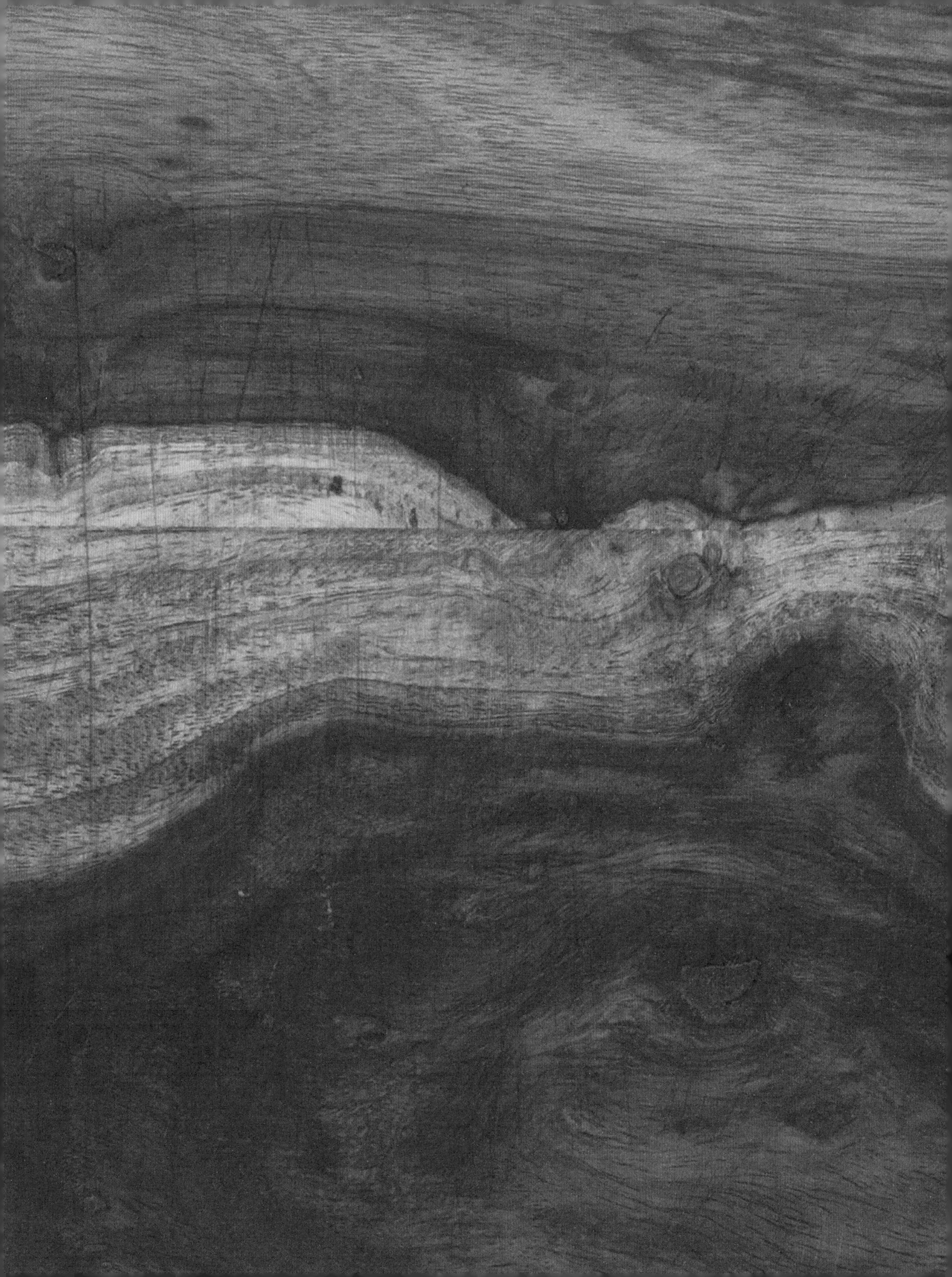

ענבים
מתוקים
9
11.99